A Brief History of
THE ROYAL NAVY IN LINCOLNSHIRE

MONSEVR. CLYNTO
GRAND. AMIRALL
DE NGLETER.

HONI SOIT QVI MAL Y PENSE

Edward Fiennes Clinton — Lord High Admiral of England 1550 – 1585

THE ROYAL NAVY IN LINCOLNSHIRE

by

E. C. Coleman

LIEUTENANT, ROYAL NAVY

RICHARD KAY

80 SLEAFORD ROAD • BOSTON • LINCOLNSHIRE • PE21 8EU

TELEPHONE: 0205 353231

The right of E. C. Coleman
to be identified as author of this work
has been asserted by him in accordance with
the Copyright Designs and Patents Act 1988

ISBN 0 902662 99 6

British Library
Cataloguing-in-Publication Data.
A catalogue record for this book is
available from the British Library

Typeset on an Apple Macintosh Plus with a LaserWrite Plus laserprinter.
Set in 12 point New Century Schoolbook typeface.

Printed by The Echo Press, Echo House, Jubilee Drive, Belton Park,
Loughborough, Leicestershire, LE11 0XS

CONTENTS

LIST OF ILLUSTRATIONS

ACKNOWLEDGMENTS

The author and the publisher gratefully acknowledge permission to publish the following illustrations. In a few instances illustrations have become available without any indication as to either the origin of the original or the source of the actual illustration used. If, despite enquiries, we have failed to identify the origin of an illustration, and it has seemed likely that it is out of copyright and in the public domain, we have used it, if it seemed that no alternative was as suitable. If we have inadvertently infringed copyright we shall be grateful if the copyright holder will contact the publisher.

Cortauld Institute, Frontispiece: Crown Copyright – Imperial War Museum, on the front cover, *HMS Lincoln, HMS Grimsby, HMS Boston,* and 43, 49, 53, 54: Maurice Hillebrandt, 45, 46, 47: *Lincolnshire Echo* (for the copies used for reproduction) 33, 34: Lincolnshire Museums, Lincolnshire County Council, Usher Gallery, 9: Museum of Lincolnshire Life, 15: Royal Marines Museum, 30: Royal Naval Submarine Museum, on the front cover the Midget Submarine, 23, 50, 51, 52: The Military Gallery, Bath, for Robert Taylor, 56. The remaining illustrations have been reproduced from photographs taken either by the author or the publisher directly or, in a few instances, from old books or isolated pictures of which the origins are unknown: if the origin is known it is credited in the caption.

GLOSSARY

BATTLE-CRUISER A heavily armed capital ship built between 1906 – 1920 which sacrificed armour for speed. Their thinly-armoured decks made them vulnerable to falling shells.

BOMB A small but strongly built vessel carrying one or more mortars. Their strength made them useful polar exploration vessels.

DESTROYER Originally 'Torpedo-boat destroyer'. A vessel built to attack enemy ships by torpedo and defend larger ships of their own fleet against enemy destroyers. Modern destroyers are as large as second world war cruisers.

FLAGSHIP An Admiral's ship. (An admiral — flag officer.)

FRIGATE Originally a fast-sailing vessel used as the 'eyes of the fleet'. Since the Second World War, a small warship capable of a variety of tasks including anti-submarine, anti-aircraft, and escort duties.

GALLEON Large, heavy, warship favoured by the 16th century Spanish navy.

LEND-LEASE Arrangement whereby the Royal Navy was loaned warships by the U.S.A. nominally in return for bases in the West Indies. Before Pearl Harbour the USA wanted to help Britain but, at the same time, did not at that stage want to become involved in the war.

LINE-OF-BATTLE SHIP 18th — 19th Century warship large enough to take its place in 'the line'. Gave rise to 'battle-ship' and 'liner'.

LORD HIGH ADMIRAL In earlier times an appointment by the Sovereign giving entire responsibility for the management and operation of the Navy. In modern times, however, the title is held by the Monarch.

NARROW SEAS Waters of the English Channel.

PRESS A means of supplying the Royal Navy with seamen. Originally a cash advance from the Sovereign for the hire of merchant ships in war but later used solely for raising seamen. Although the 'Press Gangs' finally disappeared in 1815 the system still remains as a last-resort method of manning the fleet.

PRIVATEER A privately-owned vessel authorised by the Sovereign to seek out and fight enemy ships. Often considered by the enemy to be little better than a pirate.

'Q' SHIP A warship disguised as an unarmed merchantman.

RATES From the early 17th century to the mid 19th century the Royal Navy 'rated' its ships from 1st to 6th rates. Early 'rating' depended upon the number of men carried but this later changed to the number of guns. A '1st Rate' would have over a hundred guns: a '6th Rate' twenty four.

SLOOP During the 18th and 19th centuries a shortened version of 'Sloop-of-war'. A naval vessel of less than 20 guns.

SQUADRON A number of ships, usually of the same type, under a single command.

TENDER A small vessel attendant upon a larger one.

'U' BOAT German submarine (First and Second World Wars).

COMPARATIVE RANKS

ROYAL NAVY	ROYAL NAVAL AIR SERVICE (1914 — 1918)	ARMY
Admiral of the Fleet		Field-Marshal
Admiral		General
Vice-Admiral		Lieutenant-General
Rear-Admiral		Major-General
Commodore		Brigadier
Captain		Colonel
Commander	Wing-Captain Wing-Commander	Lieutenant-Colonel
Lieutenant-Commander		Major
Lieutenant	Squadron-Commander Flight-Commander Flight-Lieutenant	Captain
Sub-Lieutenant	Flight Sub-Lieutenant	Lieutenant 2nd Lieutenant
Midshipman		Officer-Cadet

Reader! thy life, how blest so e'er it be,
Is but a voyage on a dangerous sea,
Would'st thou securely make the port of bliss,
See this brave youth: be thy great aim like his,
To live with gen'ral love by virtue's laws,
Or die with Honour in thy Country's cause.

From the memorial to:
Captain William Cust — St Wulfram's Church, Grantham.

IN THE VERY EARLY DAYS

FOR MANY YEARS before the English Navy had become the 'Royal' Navy (in the latter part of the 17th century) both seamen and the sea had made their mark upon the county of Lincolnshire. Whilst still an Anglo-Saxon kingdom, a Viking warrior idled his time away among the burned remains of Stow church by scratching an outline of his 'wave-strider' longship into the southern base of the chancel arch. It can still be seen today.

During the thirteenth century Grimsby found itself involved in the war at sea. Three shipmasters, Robert Boleham, Peter le Cogger (a 'cog' was a type of ship), and William the son of Bede, navigated ships in the fleet which sailed from Portsmouth to St Malo in 1230. In 1296 Osbert de Spaldington visited the east coast ports looking for vessels to 'press' for the king's service and, the following year, two ships — both named *Blyth de Grymmesby* — took part in Edward I's expedition to Flanders. Seventy years later, as the agents of another monarch pressed the ship of Grimsby-based Walter de Stalynburgh into service, one of the crew, John de Holand, ended up in front of the Borough Court charged with desertion.

A very different type of sailor is remembered on a memorial in Cammeringham church dedicated to Jane Tyrwhitt who, with her mother, 'were incomparable patterns to their sex'. Amongst the honored ancesters recorded on the elegant tablet is 'Sir Robert Tyrwhitt Knight and bannerette . . . Vice-Admiral to King Henry 7th'. However, as Sir Robert fails to appear in any naval records of the time he was almost certainly the receiver of a political appointment which required no knowledge or experience of ships or the sea.

When Thomas, Lord Clinton, died of the 'sweating sickness' in 1517 his five years old son, Edward Fiennes Clinton, came under the guardianship of Henry VIII. This early introduction to court circles led to his marriage at the age of eighteen to the considerably older Lady Elizabeth Talboys. His new wife was a widow who had not only been the King's mistress, but had also borne him a son, Henry Fitzroy, Duke of Richmond. None seems to have been more pleased wth this alliance than the King himself and Henry took the young Edward Clinton into his personal entourage. Consequently, he accompanied the King on foreign visits, was appointed to parliament, and was made part of the deputation sent to meet the King's new bride, Anne of Cleves. Then, perhaps because the King — tiring quickly of his new Queen (the 'Flanders Mare') — had taken a fancy yet again to the Lady Elizabeth, Clinton found himself taken to one side by the Lord High Admiral (Lord Lisle) and 'offered' a career at sea.

Serving directly under the Lord High Admiral, Clinton soon found himself in action against the Scots. Leaving his ship in the Firth of Forth he went ashore to take part in the storming of Edinburgh. His conduct on that day brought him to the attention of Edward Seymour (later the Duke of Somerset and Protector) who knighted him for his services.

Rejoining the fleet, Clinton saw action at the taking of Boulogne before being given command of his own ship by the Lord High Admiral during the repulse of a French invasion fleet.

After the death of King Henry, and the accession of the nine years old Edward VI, Clinton was given command of a fleet that was to assist the Duke of Somerset in the Duke's attempt to 'pursuade' the Scots to allow their infant Queen Mary to marry the new King of England. When the Scots refused this plan Somerset trapped their army at Musselburgh. With their backs to the sea the Scots became easy prey for Clinton's ships as they closed with the shore and opened fire on the soldiers. The English victory was not long in coming. The Scottish Queen, however, escaped to France only to meet her end, in due course, by being executed on the orders of Elizabeth I.

Clinton, meanwhile, after a voyage around the coast of Scotland destroying every Scot's ship he came across, was appointed as Governor of Boulogne – a city he bravely defended until it was returned to the French for the sum of 400,000 crowns. For this service he was raised to be Lord High Admiral, the previous holder of that post, Lisle – now the Duke of Northumberland – being too busy removing the head of the Duke of Somerset.

The following year Clinton was elected a Knight of the Garter, made Governor of the Tower of London, and appointed Lord-Lieutenant of Lincolnshire.

The nimble footwork he had demonstrated in keeping on the right side of both Somerset and Northumberland was to come in most useful again when 'Bloody' Mary took over the throne from the Northumberland-sponsored Lady Jane Grey. Despite losing his job as Lord High Admiral Clinton was soon to be seen at the fore-front of the forces putting down a rebellion raised in favour of Lady Jane. Within four years he had managed to take over the post of Lord High Admiral again, achieving a great victory over the French at Conquet.

On the death of Mary, Clinton could have been excused for thinking that his support for that queen might have damaged his interest with the new one – the strongly Protestant Elizabeth. But Elizabeth knew better than to deprive herself of a proven leader and kept Clinton as her Lord High Admiral. In return he helped command the English army which crushed a powerful rising in the north of the country and personally took charge of the fleet with Elizabeth's order '. . . to sink at once, and without question, any French vessel he might find carrying troops to Scotland . . .' It was a critical period in the Queen's reign and for his diligence in carrying out his duties Clinton was 'advanced to the dignity' of Earl of Lincoln on 4 May 1572.

Although he did not take personal command at sea again Clinton supervised the organisation of the fledgling Elizabethan navy and helped make firm the foundations of, what was later to become, the Royal Navy.

He died in January 1585 and is buried in St George's chapel, Windsor, having survived – despite being perilously close to the crown – under four monarchs.

For many centuries 'interest' – the good fortune of being 'well connected' – played a vital part in any young man's career if he wished to serve at sea. Few could have had greater 'interest' than London born Robert Bertie, the eldest son of Peregrine, Baron Willoughby de Beck and Eresby, for his godmother was no less than Queen Elizabeth I, whilst his godfathers were the Earls of Essex and Leicester. Having proved to be a keen student in world affairs he was allowed to join his godfathers in their 1597 expedition against Cadiz. During the capture of the city Bertie so distinguished himself that he was knighted in the market-place at the age of sixteen. Remaining on the continent he took part in the 1598 siege of Amiens before visiting many of the capital cities of Europe. When he found this extension to his education becoming a little too boring he would vary his routine by joining an English ship sailing off to hunt down the Spaniards. In this way he learned the art of seamanship and was present at the capture of several Spanish galleons.

On the death of his father Bertie succeeded to the Barony but was dismayed to find that the Lincolnshire estate at Grimsthorpe was in very poor order with several large outstanding debts (his father, as the Lord General of the English forces in the Netherlands, had complained bitterly of the costs he was personally forced to meet to keep his soldiers fed and clothed: '. . . I am so straitly scanted and of mine own spent myself so near the bones that I am not able to do anything . . .'). Accordingly, he applied to James I for permission to remain abroad in an effort to raise enough money to settle his father's debts. Unusually, when his background is considered, he opted to study commerce rather than seek his fortune as a mercenary in foreign military conflicts and proved so successful that he was soon able to return to Grimsthorpe where he improved the estate '. . . by noble traffic, he having learned at Venice and Florence that merchandise is consistent with nobility . . .' It also helped that he managed to make a 'rich match' with Lord Montague of Boughton's daughter Elizabeth, and managed to wrest from his mother's relations the office of Lord High Chamberlain. Having been made a Knight of the Bath in 1605 he spent the next nineteen years managing his estate, in particular draining 36,000 acres of fens of which he was allowed to keep 24,000 for himself, much to the distress of other Lincolnshire landowners who had refused to back his enterprise.

Called by his monarch to serve his country he spent a short time in Greece as ambassador prior to being sent to the Low Countries as colonel of a regiment of 1,500 men. Again he was not there for long when he was recalled to take part in naval expeditions led by the Duke of Buckingham, demonstrating throughout that he had lost none of his early promise. Indeed, so much did he impress by his handling of his ships that, on his return he was created Earl of Lindsey.

In August 1628 the Duke of Buckingham – the Lord High Admiral – opened the front door of his house in Portsmouth to find himself facing John

Felton, a disgruntled ex-army officer, who plunged his knife into the Duke killing him instantly. As Buckingham's second in command for the forthcoming expedition for the relief of Rochelle the Earl of Lindsey might have expected to have succeeded to the title of Lord High Admiral but, in an act that was to become standard for later generations of naval administrators, the office of Lord High Admiral was placed 'in commission' and the work undertaken by a number of 'Commissioners'. This step was not simply a means of producing a better organisation for the Navy but also a method of ensuring that Buckingham's widow should continue to receive the advantages that went with the position. It also may have led to the failure of the expedition, for Lindsey, despite being made Admiral for the duration, did not have the authority to impress himself over the 'character of the officers' (the captains had claimed that their ships were in no condition to force a boom that had been thrown across the harbour mouth – the following day Rochelle surrendered to the French with the fleet looking on as bad weather caused waves so large that they smashed the boom). Perhaps to compensate for this slight to his obvious claim to the post Lindsey was made a Knight of the Garter in 1630 and given command of a fleet to secure the 'Narrow Seas' (i.e. the English Channel) for the English King. This was followed by command of perhaps the most notorious fleet ever to be assembled in England's naval history. This was the 'Ship Money' fleet whose financing was eventually to lead to the death of the monarch. Three years later, in 1639, Lindsey was appointed as the governor of Berwick in the face of the Scots taking up arms against the English.

With the outbreak of the Civil War, Lindsey raised men for the King's cause in Lincolnshire and Nottingham, the gentlemen of those counties supporting the King 'chiefly from their strong regard for the Earl of Lindsey'. Eventually, King Charles appointed the Earl as commander-in-chief of all the royal forces. But there was a very large flaw in this, otehwise supreme, honour. Prince Rupert had been made General of the Horse and in his commission a clause had been inserted stating that the Prince would take orders from no-one other than the King himself. Matters came to a head on 23 October 1642, at the Battle of Edgehill when despite requests from Lindsey to the contrary Prince Rupert led a wild, but pointless, cavalry charge at the parliamentary forces. Once he learned that the Prince had '. . . set out without advising him, and in a form he liked not . . .' Lindsey declared that '. . . if he was not fit to be a general he would at least die a colonel at the head of his regiment . . .' At this he dismounted from his horse, took up a long pike, and advanced against the enemy at the head of his old regiment. It was to be his last act. He was to die before the following morning of wounds received in the battle, his loss 'a great grief to the army, and generally to all who knew him'. Robert Bertie, the First Earl of Lindsey, lies buried in Edenham church, the plaque recording his achievements supported by crossed anchors recalling his long and distinguished service at sea.

Another memorial in Edenham church was raised to mark the burial place

1. Detail from the Earl of Lindsey's Tomb in Edenham Church.

of one of the First Earl of Lindsey's great-grandsons. The Honourable Norreys Bertie. He had made several voyages as a 'Voluntier' (trainee officer) during the reign of James II. After the 'Glorious Revolution' of 1688 he joined the army and served as Guidon of the Guards (standard bearer) during their campaigns in Flanders. Two years later he 'went a Voluntier' on board the *Suffolk* under the command of Admiral Russell (whose orders contained the somewhat self-protective instruction – 'If the Admiral, or any flagship, should be in distress, and make the usual signal, the ships in the fleet are to endeavour to get up close into line, between him and the enemy, as they can; having always an eye to defend him, if the enemy should come to annoy him in that condition').

Unfortunately, Norreys Bertie was not to have the opportunity to come to his admiral's aid for, having just been promoted lieutenant, the ship called at Dartmouth where he 'fell ill of a malignant fever' and died aged 'about 25 years'.

When the Earl of Lindsey was made Admiral of the 'Ship Money' fleet his Vice-Admiral was Sir William Monson who had been born the third son of Sir John Monson in the small village of South Carlton, just north-west of the city of Lincoln. Monson began his sea career in 1585 as a 'common sailor' on board a small merchantman. When in company with another, equally small, vessel the two ships came across a much larger (300 ton) Spanish ship. Despite the Spaniard being well armed and manned the English seamen decided to board her in an attempt at capture. By late evening the two English ships had managed to place themselves on either side of the Spaniard and as many men as could be spared clambered up her sides. The Spaniards retreated below decks firing their pistols up through the hatch combings. Forcing their way down through the decks, and having to fight for every inch the English seamen failed to notice that the weather had begun to worsen. Eventually, those remaining on the attacking ships were forced to ungrapple their vessels and stand off leaving their shipmates stranded on the

2.The Hon. Norreys Bertie's bust in Edenham Church.

Spaniard. The fighting continued all night with the Spaniards repeatedly attempting to blow up their own decks with the English above them. Finally, at about seven the following morning, the Spaniards surrendered. Monson later wrote: 'When we came to take a view of our people we found few left alive but could shew a wound or shot through their cloaths in that fight.' He was sixteen years old at the time and had taken part in the capture of the first Spanish ship ever taken by the English and brought home as a prize.

Two years after that incident Monson was given his own merchant ship to command and he undertook a voyage to the Canary Islands. For various reasons (the captain's inexperience amongst them) the ship was far longer away from port than had been intended and when they reached the coast of Ireland they were reduced to their last biscuit. In the following year (1588) he was to be found in the Queen's service onboard the pinnace *Charles* fighting against the Spanish Armada. The remainder of his life was to be in the service of his country.

Within twelve months of the Armada action he was given command of his own royal ship – the *Margret* – on an expedition led by the Earl of Cumberland which led to the capture of several valuable French, Spanish and Portuguese ships. Again, due to failing to obtain water at the Canaries, and having supplied Sir Francis Drake's ships as Drake returned from an attack on Cadiz, the ship's companies suffered terrible privations. Monson wrote, 'The extremity we endured was more terrible than befel any ship in the eighteen years' war . . . for sixteen days together we never tasted a drop of drink, either beer, wine, or water'. The only liquid that was available was vinegar which was rationed out at three spoonfuls per day. Some men died from drinking sea water. Upon his safe return Monson was so ill that he had to remain on shore for a year to recover.

When (in 1591) Cumberland mounted a further expedition he took Monson as the captain of his own ship. Unfortunately, during an engagement with a Portuguese fleet (and with Cumberland directing affairs from another ship) Monson found himself surrounded by six enemy galleys. Despite a desperate fight Monson was captured and spent much of the next two years as a prisoner in Lisbon castle. Whilst imprisoned he was instrumental in helping a fellow prisoner escape, but the man's recapture led to Monson being under threat of execution and only managing to escape death by insisting that, as a prisoner of war, he owed no loyalty to his gaolers.

Upon his release in 1593 Monson returned to his earlier post as captain of Cumberland's ship (the *Golden Lion*) this time leading eight other vessels in an expedition against enemy shipping off the Azores. They gained some success and managed to more than cover the cost of the enterprise but the most memorable incident appears to have been when Monson, left isolated by Cumberland and with a number of captured ships in his charge, was suddenly attacked by a far superior Spanish force and found himself scrambling down the side of one ship whilst the enemy swarmed up the other. The incident severely injured his leg and caused him to be partially lame for the remainder of his life. This incident did not prevent him, on a serious illness overtaking Cumberland, from going ashore on a Portuguese island and (no doubt employing some Portuguese langugage learned in prison) managing to save his leader's life by the use of 'threats and promises of reward' to secure a cow from which fresh milk could be obtained.

After marrying in 1595 Monson was given command of the *Allsides* and sailed from Plymouth as second in command to Cumberland in the *Malice Scourge*. They were not long out of harbour when Cumberland left his ship in command of another captain and returned to shore with no intention of returning. Monson, furious that he had not been consulted about this new arrangement which appeared to place him under the authority of a captain he neither knew nor cared about, promptly took off over the horizon and 'betook myself off to my own adventure'. Such an action saw no results against the enemy and lost him the valuable friendship of Cumberland.

His next exploit was to expose further his ablity to over-react to events – a side of his nature which came close to bringing him disaster later in his career. Appointed to command the *Repulse*, the Earl of Essex's flagship, and with Lord Charles Howard, the Earl of Nottingham, as Lord High Admiral in the *Ark Royal*, Monson took part in an expedition to Cadiz. Upon their arrival Monson pressed urgently upon Essex that he must concentrate upon the ships in the harbour rather than attacking the town. His reasoning was that the treasure on the ships could not be removed and that the captured ships could be taken home to England where they would 'always be before men's eyes there, and put them in mind of the greatness of the exploit'. But an attack on the town would be 'probably not long enjoyed, and quickly forgotten'. Essex, however, had other ideas and landed with three regiments. To make matters worse, Monson saw the Lord High Admiral who, perhaps, feeling 'a little eclipsed' followed Essex ashore with landing parties of seamen. Little came of the venture and Monson wasted no time in telling anybody who cared to listen that if only he had been listened to the outcome would have been very different. He seemed to care little that such behaviour can quickly create enemies. Nevertheless, despite his outbursts, Essex knighted him in the Queen's name for his conduct during the actual fighting – Monson's sword hilt had been shattered by a musket ball as it hung by his side.

Perhaps because of his outspoken behaviour Monson did not get another command until three years later when he was appointed to the *Rainbow* during a further expedition to the Azores. Again he lost no time in telling the expedition leader (Essex) how he should conduct the battle. Yet again he was ignored and when Essex failed to achieve the number of enemy captures that Monson had hoped for he again loudly found 'fault with the general for his want of seamanship and arrangement'.

In 1599 Monson transferred to the *Defiance* and took his place in a fleet which had been assembled under the Lord High Admiral. The fleet had been brought together for the purpose of defending the country from a suspected Spanish attempt to land troops in England. When that threat did not materialise he was appointed as Vice-Admiral on the *Garland* under Sir Richard Lawson on the *Repulse*. Clearly Monson could work with Lawson as they finished their voyage by capturing an enemy vessel valued at two hundred thousand pounds. On his return Monson was ordered to take command of a squadron of six ships (with himself on the *Swiftsure*) to find out if the Portugese and Spaniards were mounting an expedition against Ireland, Nothing was found and, generally, the voyage was a disappointment high-lighted only by a savage engagement with a Spanish galleon off Cape St. Vincent where the gunfire 'rent his ship, so that a team of oxen might have crept through under the half-deck; and one shot killed seven men.' On another occasion he managed to save his ship during an enemy pursuit '. . . resolving not to see a pinnace of Her Majesty's so lost if he could rescue her with the loss of his life . . .' Shortening sail in order that the Spaniard should catch up and give him the chance to go down fighting he was amazed (and no doubt gratified) to see the far more powerful enemy vessel also shorten sail. His action had clearly confused the Spanish captain who, far from finding an easy victory, now found himself in a position of having to face up to an English foe clearly intending to slug it out to the last round. With the Spaniard having 'lost weigh' Monson crammed on more sail and fled with both his life and his ship intact.

On his return from his duties off the Spanish and Portugese coasts he was appointed again as Lawson's Vice-Admiral although this time in a larger ship — the *Mer Honour* — than the Admiral himself. This peculiar arrangement had been brought about due to the fact that there was a suspicion that Lawson might oppose the arrival of James VI of Scotland as he took the throne of England as James I. Should there be any sign of revolt from Lawson, Monson was to race into harbour, collect the Lord High Admiral and then take over Lawson's ship. However, in the outcome, Lawson proved to be loyal and the plan was never put into action.

In July Monson was appointed Admiral of the Narrow Seas, a position he held for twelve years. He started badly by outraging the Dutch who, having been under Spanish domination for many years, were out for revenge against their former masters. Whenever a Spanish vessel sailed into the English Channel or the North Sea they came under the threat of Dutch attack. Monson, trying to keep the peace in his area of responsibility, persuaded King James to issue a proclamation prohibiting '. . . all nations from offering violence to one another . . .' whilst sailing through the Narrow Seas. This outraged the Dutch who, in an early testing of this proclamation, found themselves facing Monson's guns and having to withdraw,

Another group who came under Monson's jurisdiction was the pirates who sailed out of Broad Haven, County Mayo. In an effort to rid his area of these unwelcome seafarers Monson disguised his ship and his crew as fellow pirates. He was received by the real pirates '. . . and still more their women, with open arms: and in feasting, drinking, dancing, and love-making the days passed merrily . . .'. Once he was sure that everyone's guard was down, Monson seized all the pirate leaders and held them for twenty-four hours with his prisoners existing in full expectation of being hanged in the very near future. To their astonishment (perhaps in repayment of their lavish hospitality) Monson released them under the threat of hanging if they did not improve their ways. Only one pirate was hung – a renegade Englishman. Monson would not tolerate treason. After that raid it was said that the pirates '. . . in a little time wholly abandoned Ireland'.

Whilst Monson was away at sea, the enemies he had made through being so outspoken began to work against him. Their moment came when a number of unfortunate events combined against him. He had always been of the belief that England's navy was her most important asset and he constantly raged against abuses which began to creep in 'like rust into iron'. Eventually he managed to have a Commission raised to enquire into these abuses but, in doing so, only managed to anger the Lord High Admiral and his high-born friends. At about the same time that he was annoying his superiors by threatening their 'fringe benefits' he was given orders to intercept and arrest the popular Lady Arabella Seymour as she fled to France. This lady was the English-born cousin of James I who many of the English felt had a better claim to the throne than her Scottish relative. She had been suspected of being involved in the plot against the throne which had led to the execution of Sir Walter Raleigh and did nothing to improve her status with the King when it was found out that she was becoming romantically involved with William Seymour, Lord Beauchamp, whose family were seen as possible pretenders to the throne through their connection with Lady Jane Seymour – one of Henry VIII's wives. When the King heard that Lady Arabella was about to become engaged to Seymour (thirteen years her junior) he had them brought into his presence and personally forbade the union. Despite this. the two were married secretly and, when he found out, James had Lady Arabella put under the care of the Bishop of Durham and had Seymour thrown into the Tower of London. Many people throughout the country were outraged at this action and all would have cheered to have heard that Lady Arabella had escaped from her guardians dressed as a man and taken a ship to France, whilst the following day Seymour changed clothes with his barber and made his escape from the Tower and followed in his wife's wake across the Channel. Unfortunately for both of them, just as she was within four miles of Calais, Monson hove to, stopped her ship and took off Lady Arabella. The King, by now thoroughly annoyed by his cousin's actions, had her locked in the Tower where she died four years later. Monson, despite only carrying out his orders, '. . . incurred the hatred of many for his share in the business.'

Monson's luck continued to hold against him when he ordered one of his ships to fire against a Dutch vessel which had failed to strike its topsail in salute to the English flag (as was required of all foreign vessels in the Narrow Seas). Unfortunately the ship was carrying the Dutch Ambassador on board who complained bitterly to the King on his arrival in England. Finally his elder brother, Sir Thomas, was held in the Tower accused of treason. Monson quickly followed him. It took six months to clear his name and it was twenty years before he was appointed to sea again. This was the 'Ship Money' fleet commanded by the Earl of Lindsey. Monson viewed the job as Vice-Admiral to Lindsey as a great honour particularly as he was a firm supporter of the highly unpopular tax believing that the defence of the country outweighed any constitutional niceties involving differences between King and Parliament. He was, no doubt, correct in his view concerning defence as a combined French and Dutch fleet had assembled off Portland '. . . in the bragging pretence of questioning His Majesty's prerogative on the Narrow Seas'. Upon learning that the English fleet was at sea the combined fleet broke up and headed for home. The English fleet, as Monson recorded, '. . . made good our seas and shores, gave laws to our neighbour nations, and restored the ancient

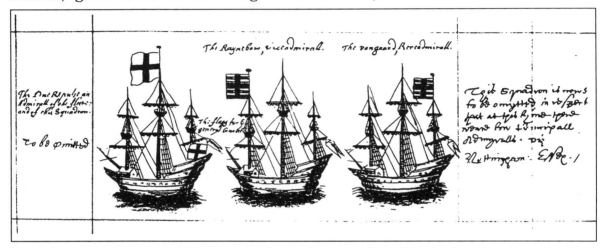

3. Ships' signals at the attack on Cadiz.
Monson commanded the 'Repulse' and was later to command the 'Rainbow'.

sovereignty of the Narrow Seas to our gracious King'. It was a noble end to a long, and often painful, career in the service of his country.

Sir William Monson spent the final eight years of his life writing his memoirs – 'Monson's Naval Tracts' – partly to clear his name of some of the accusations that had been levelled against him but, for the most part, explaining the life and works of the navies of Elizabeth, James I, and Charles I. In them he revealed that his pay at sea had started at ten shillings per month and ended at forty shillings a day (plus the right to have sixteen footmen in his retinue).

He also viewed the newly-fashionable use of the 'prospective glass' (telescope) with a jaundiced eye. Weak ships, he claimed, would be able to fool a stronger vessel by mounting man-sized dummies on its upper deck and carrying mock cannons made of wood '. . . which the glass cannot discern from iron . . .' (Such deceptions became common-place in the eighteenth century, the wooden cannon being known as 'Quakers'). The captain of a strong warship, on the other hand, should '. . . stow his men save so many as may sail the ship, in [his] hold and embolden the other [enemy] to come near him . . .' – a ruse adopted by 'Q' ships against U-Boats during the First World War.

Having completed his works (invaluable to subsequent naval historians) he died in February 1642, aged seventy-two and is buried at St. Martin's-in-the-Field, London.

John Smith of Willoughby, born in 1580, attended Louth Grammar School before sailing away as a young man to Italy in a ship crowded with French pilgrims. One way to reduce the overcrowding was to throw overboard anyone suspected of being a Hugenot. Consequently, Smith found himself swimming in the Mediterranean only to be picked up shortly afterwards by a pirate ship. Having convinced his new hosts that he was a good seaman and, therefore, of some value, he served with them until he was able to escape and make his way back to England. Eventually, as 'Captain' Smith, he was chosen to lead an expedition to the New World where he explored the coasts of Chesapeake Bay and the Potomac and Rappahonnack rivers. During this period he managed to upset the local Indian Chief, Powhatan, who, when he was just about to dispatch Smith to the Happy Hunting Grounds with a large club, was stopped by his beautiful daughter, Pocohontas. The Indian princess, it seems, had formed an attachment to the English sea captain. As a result, Smith did the honourable thing, and arranged to have one of his officers marry the Indian princess before founding the state of Virginia with its capital, Jamestown, virtually single-handed.

4. Captain John Smith.

The font in which John Smith was baptised can still be seen in Willoughby church beneath a stained glass window from which a rather stern-looking Pocohontas gazes down. On the same wall a plaque has been erected to the memory of John Smith by the Jamestown Foundation and The Commonwealth of Virginia. On one side of the plaque flies the Stars and Stripes, on the other, the Virginia state flag.

The colonies begun by Smith and others on the east coast of America attracted men and women who felt stifled in their religious beliefs. Amongst the earliest to attempt to begin a new life across the Atlantic was a community of families from around the village of Scrooby in the neighbouring county of Nottinghamshire. In mid-September, 1607, the group set out towards a point near Boston known as Fishtoft Gowt (now known as Scotia Creek). Waiting for them was a Dutch ship they had chartered to take them over to Holland (from where eventually they would find a vessel to take them to the colonies). But the captain of the ship had betrayed them and they were handed over to the authorities at Boston. Seven of the leaders were put into cells in Boston Guildhall, (the cells can still be seen to this day). But the idea did not die. The following year another attempt was to be more successful. The men travelled on foot to Immingham whilst their womenfolk and children sailed down the Trent from Gainsborough. However, the women and children's boat became stuck on a mudbank and the waiting Dutch vessel promptly fled with just the husbands and fathers on board when an armed body of men was seen heading towards the pick-up point. The families were to be re-united after some months had passed. Twelve years later they stepped on to the soil of the New World, free to worship in their own way. Amongst other early settlers was the Sempringham born Lady Arbella Fiennes Clinton, the daughter of Thomas, the Earl of Lincoln, and grand-daughter of Edward Fiennes Clinton.

The above Engraving, from a Drawing by Pocock, represents a View of the Lady Banks, a ship built for the East Country Trade, at Boston, Lincolnshire; taken from a sawpit in the Builder's Yard. Boston Steeple in the distance. From a Drawing by W. Brand, Esq. of Boston.

5. This engraving is taken from 'A Biographical Memoir of Thomas (Hoar) Bertie, Esq., Rear Admiral of the White Squadron. [Naval Chronicle Vol. XXVI] It illustrates the former significance of Boston as a shipbuilding port.

In many ways Boston was the most obvious port from which to begin a sea voyage from the eastern part of England. Not only was it one of the premier ports on the east coast with easy access to the Low Countries, but its importance had been recognised by Queen Elizabeth by a Charter of 10 February 1575, in which she granted the port its own 'Court of Admiralty'. This meant that all matters concerning the sea and rivers in an area bounded by Wainfleet Haven to the north and the borders of Norfolk to the south (and including as geographical limits such exotic sounding places as 'Pullyheads', 'Knoke', and 'Doggesheade in the Foote',) were exempt from the jurisdiction of the Lord High Admiral. The port's own Court of Admiralty — to be held every Wednesday — was presided over by the Mayor and a judge and could deal with every matter arising from problems at sea in their area (excluding piracy and robbery) and even matters affecting Boston that occurred 'beyond the sea'. This useful source of fines and taxes came to an end with the introduction of the Municipal Corporations Act of 1835.

The Civil war saw little naval activity in the area with the main incident being a landing by royalist ships of Cavaliers at Skegness — most of whom were promptly captured by local Parliamentarians. However, as Cromwell's first battle had taken place at Belton, just north of Grantham, it was decided to name a ship in honour of the event. The 30-gun *Grantham* was built at Southampton in 1654. With the restoration of the monarchy it was felt inappropriate to keep the name so the ship was re-christened as the *Garland* (the name *Grantham* re-appeared between 1787-1792 as a 'slop' [stores] ship). The Dutch wars provided a worrying time with Dutch privateers roaming off the Lincolnshire coast swooping on every unguarded vessel and causing such concern by closing with the shore that local farm hands had to be used to help troops guarding the coastline. Their ability to get in so close was due to the shallow draught of their vessels, designed for the waters around Holland.

Among those who decided to do something about this threat was Edward Fane of Fulbeck who went to sea as a 'Gentleman Volunteer' in 1666. This was particularly bad timing as, on the first of June that year, he found himself on board one of fifty-six English ships about to engage eighty five of the enemy. With neither side wanting to give way the battle raged for four days, the ships separating only when darkness fell and to hold church services. (The naval 'Church pennant' still flown today, carries the English and Dutch colours in memory of this battle.) Eventually the Dutch retired, their ships shattered and with shot-lockers empty, but the English had suffered more. Eight thousand English seamen had been killed or wounded and seventeen ships – including two flagships – had been lost. Despite being involved in such a gruelling and bloody example of dogged tenacity (unequalled in naval warfare before or since) Edward Fane never lost the thirst for adventure and, as his monument in Fulbeck church records, 'after visiting Jerusalem and other parts dyed at London Dec Ye 15th 1679 aged 37'.

Another 'Gentleman Volunteer' was Charles Mordaunt – later to be the third Earl of Peterborough. Well connected with the naval hierarchy he went to sea at the age of sixteen and managed to prove extremely unpopular with the 'tarpaulin' captains (men who had entered the navy as seamen and had worked their way up). They accused him of 'committing villanies of all sort and debauching the poor seamen' (in later writing he claimed to have committed three capital offences before he was twenty). So bad was his reputation that when he again volunteered to go to sea in 1681, his application was refused despite his being well-connected (his uncle was a Vice-Admiral). His response was to buy his own ship, a 45 gun fourth rate which he named *Loyall Mordaunt*, and to get involved whether anyone else liked it or not. He went into politics in 1687 only returning to the sea in command of a Dutch squadron in opposition to King James. Further political intrigue brought him, in 1702, the Governorship of Jamaica along with the role of Commander-in-Chief of 'all the ships of war employed on that station'. But when he found that he was likely to be engaged in fighting the Spaniards he declared himself to be 'no worker of miracles' and he declined. Four years later he found himself selected as 'Joint Admiral' with Sir Clowdiseley Shovell for operations against the Spanish off Barcelona (an extremely rare appointment since he had not come through the ranks normally required to reach such an august post, only one other person had been so appointed – the Duke of York). As it was, things turned out well because Peterborough (as he had now become) left the nautical aspects of the campaign to the experienced Sir Clowdiseley (a tarpaulin of the old school) whilst he concentrated on the fighting ashore. So successful was this arrangement that the old concept of 'Joint Admirals' (a system developed from the ancient policy of 'Councils of War') was never used again.

Whilst the war was still in progress Peterborough decided to visit the Duke of Savoy, taking passage in the 70 gun *Resolution* (Captain Sir Henry Mordaunt – his son). They were being escorted by the *Enterprise* and the *Milford* when a French Squadron of six heavily armed ships hoved into sight and began to close. Peterborough rapidly transfered himself to the faster *Enterprise* and, taking the *Milford* as an escort, left his son to face the enemy alone whilst he reached Leghorn safely. Sir Henry fought a gallant rearguard action, eventually being driven ashore where he fended off repeated attacks attempting to set fire to his ship. The following morning, with the *Resolution* clearly beyond recovery, he unloaded the ship's stores, landed all his men safely, and then fired the vessel himself. He was to die within two years as a result of the wounds he had received in the action. His father lived for another twenty-seven years becoming the first Peer of the Realm to marry a lady of the stage (the singer Anastasia Robinson). This did not stop him ardently pursuing a mistress of George II 'a deaf woman of forty'. His portrait with its naval trappings – telescopes, cannons, and ship in the background – looks down into the Great Hall of Burghley House, near Stamford.

One man who would have greatly disapproved of the Earl's conduct was Samuel Wesley, father of John Wesley the founder of Methodism, chaplain to one of His Majesty's men-of-war. Probably finding that his rate of pay (four-pence per month from each member of the ship's company) to be insufficient to support a wife he left to take up a curacy and get married. Six years later he became the Rector of Epworth and, when his rectory was burned down by a disgruntled congregation, had it rebuilt using ship's timbers taken from vessels being broken up at Gainsborough. (In 1990 the warden at the Old Rectory maintained the naval connection – having survived the sinking of *HMS Coventry* during the Second World War).

In an attempt to protect merchant shipping from enemy attack during the early years of the 18th century, Royal Naval vessels were based along the east coast. *HMS Woolf*, a tiny 2 gun sloop, was stationed at Grimsby in 1703 when a message came that a French privateer (a privately owned warship) had attacked a convoy off the entrance to the Humber. *Woolf* immediately put to sea and bore down on the offender who prepared to fight or flee. However, English prisoners on board the Frenchman decided the matter by throwing overboard two of their captors – the remainder surrendering to the *Woolf* who brought them and their ship back into Grimsby. The following year the French gained their revenge by capturing the *Woolf* and using it against its previous owners until 1708 when the ship was retaken by the English.

TECHNOLOGY IMPROVES IN XVIII CENTURY

WHEN YOUNG John Harrison moved from Pontifract to Barrow-on-Humber about 1696 it was fully expected that he would continue with his father's trade as a carpenter. But, having acquired a high degree of skill in wood-working, he began to take an intense interest in clock making. The result was a series of wooden clocks that proved extremely successful, particularly when employed in church towers. Learning, in 1714, that the Commissioners of the Board of Longitude were offering prizes up to the value of £20,000 for a time-keeper that could be used to fix longitude at sea, Harrison accepted the challenge (latitude could be fixed accurately by sighting the sun, but longitude depended upon an accuracy in time-keeping hitherto not available). Not only had the clock to be far more accurate than anything previously designed, but it also had to be rugged enough to withstand a sea-voyage through a considerable temperature range. By 1728 Harrison had produced a design suitable for submission to the Board. Seven years later a working model underwent trials on the Humber followed by a voyage to Lisbon and back on board *HMS Centurion*. Its accuracy had proved to be amazing, so much so that the Admiralty forbade its continued use at sea in case, with the country at war, it should fall into the hands of the enemy (the clock itself ran for a further thirty years without being stopped for cleaning or oiling.) A second time-keeper was produced to improve on the sea-keeping

6. *John Harrison*

qualities of the first. There was no doubting its accuracy but, this time, the Admiralty would not even allow sea-trials for fear of losing it to the enemy. A third time-keeper was produced by Harrison that had taken seventeen years to design and make and contained 753 moving parts. It was, however, to be his fourth time-keeper that proved to be the breakthrough the Board of Longitude had been searching for. Resembling a large pocket watch 'No 4' was taken on board *HMS Deptford* in 1761 for a voyage to Jamaica via Madeira. Upon arrival it was found that the time-keeper had lost just five seconds resulting in an error of less than one geographical mile (the Board had been hoping for

*7a. From The Historical
Chronicle: July 1737*

*7b. Harrison's first chronometer – although extremely
accurate it was somewhat inconveniently bulky and
weighed 72 lbs.*

*7c. Harrison's fourth timepiece which
lost only five seconds on a voyage to
Jamaica.*

*7d. The chronometer used on Cook's
second voyage: mechanically an exact
replica of Harrison's fourth timepiece.*

anything less than an error of 30 nautical miles). Until now the Commissioners had been putting off the payment of the reward and it still took the intervention of George III ('By God, Harrison, I'll see you righted!') and a second trial on board *HMS Tartar* before they sent any money to the, by now almost blind, Harrison. Even then they underpaid him by £1,250. When, in the 1920's, after years of neglect, his time-keepers were restored, the restorer likened the work to 'trying to thread a needle stuck into the tailboard of a motor-lorry which you are chasing on a bicycle'. Harrison's portrait, with him holding his fourth time-keeper, can be seen in Barrow-on-Humber church and a plaque in the village marks the site of his home.

The ability to be able to navigate with a high degree of precision was not high on the list of reasons why service in the Royal Navy failed to attract the seamen of Grimsby. Regardless of a measure of protection under the law, fishermen, being hardy and experienced seamen were always sought out by the press gangs. *HMS Salamander* sent a gang ashore in 1739 which was shortly followed by a lieutenant from *HMS Greenwich* seeking the Mayor of Grimsby's 'backing' (literally signing the back of his Press Warrant) in the search for deserters. On such occasions the Mayor had two choices – support the gang and add his authority to the search, or (in a desperate bid to retain popularity with the voters) refuse to back the warrant and have to deal with the riot which often followed a raid by the Press Gang. In 1756 *HMS Frederick's* press gang grabbed, among others, Matthew Empson, a Grimsby seamen. It was to be twelve years before he managed to gain his release.

AN EIGHTEENTH CENTURY CAPTAIN

William Cust was born in London, the second son of Sir Richard Cust and his wife Anne (née Brownlowe). Having decided upon a life at sea he 'passed for' Lieutenant in June 1741 and served for the next four years onboard the *Royal George* (whilst his elder brother, Sir John, became member of parliament for Grantham). In January 1746 he was appointed as commander of the sloop-of-war *Otter* in which he spent most of his time in pursuit of French privateers. The high point of this period of his life came in July 1747 when he chased the heavily armed (eighteen-gun) privateer *Vigilante* into St Malo harbour (not Cherbourg as his memorial plaque was later to state), The *Vigilante* anchored beneath the guns of the harbour fortress in the belief that she was safe and had shaken off her pursuer. But Commander Cust was of a different belief. Bringing the *Otter* into the harbour he lowered his ship's boats and led his seamen in boarding the *Vigilante*. Within a very short time the ship was in English hands and, disregarding the cannonading that had broken out from the fort, sailed the ship out of the harbour followed closely by his own ship.

Upon his safe arrival back in Plymouth Cust was promoted Captain and appointed to the *Boston* – a twenty-four-gun frigate – being built in the New England town for service on the America station. When he arrived to take up his new command he reported to the area admiral, Rear-Admiral Knowles, from whom he learned that an attack was to be mounted against Port Louis,

Hispaniola (Haiti). Having gained the admiral's permission to join the expedition he went on board the *Elizabeth* to serve for the duration of the attack under the command of her captain. This brave action was to be his undoing for as the *Elizabeth* led the attack and closed with the enemy Captain Cust, behaving 'with uncommon presence of mind in the heat of the battle, . . . his Family and Country were at once deprived of a great honour and ornament to both'. The twenty-eight years old captain had been struck by a cannon-ball.

He is remembered by a plaque surmounted by a bust in St Wulfram's church, Grantham. Oddly, however – in addition to getting the place of his greatest feat wrong – the plaque gives the date of his death as 'Mar: 8, 1747' – exactly one year before he actually died – in 1748.

8a. Captain William Cust's memorial in St. Wulfram's Church, Grantham.

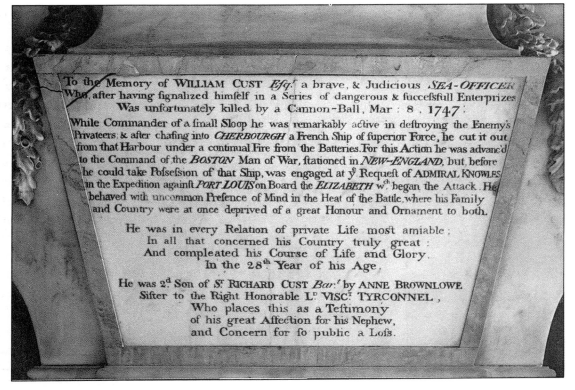

To the Memory of WILLIAM CUST *Esq.* a brave, & Judicious *SEA-OFFICER* Who, after having signalized himself in a Series of dangerous & successfull Enterprizes Was unfortunately killed by a Cannon-Ball, Mar : 8, 1747 : While Commander of a small Sloop he was remarkably active in destroying the Enemy's Privateers; & after chasing into *CHERBOURGH* a French Ship of superior Force, he cut it out from that Harbour under a continual Fire from the Batteries. For this Action he was advanc'd to the Command of the *BOSTON* Man of War, stationed in *NEW-ENGLAND*, but, before he could take Possession of that Ship, was engaged at y° Request of ADMIRAL KNOWLES in the Expedition against *PORT LOUIS* on Board the *ELIZABETH* w.ch began the Attack. He behaved with uncommon Presence of Mind in the Heat of the Battle, where his Family and Country were at once deprived of a great Honour and Ornament to both.

He was in every Relation of private Life most amiable ; In all that concerned his Country truly great : And compleated his Course of Life and Glory. In the 28.th Year of his Age.

He was 2.d Son of S.r RICHARD CUST *Bar.t* by ANNE BROWNLOWE, Sister to the Right Honorable L.D VISC.T TYRCONNEL , Who places this as a Testimony of his great Affection for his Nephew, and Concern for so public a Loss.

8b. Detail from William Cust's memorial above.

LINCOLNSHIRE AND AUSTRALIA
BANKS, FLINDERS, AND OTHERS

DESPITE BEING BORN in London, Joseph Banks spent much of his life (particularly the autumn of each year) at the family estate at Revesby, between Boston and Horncastle. The estate had been purchased by his great-grandfather who departed this life by falling off his roof 'while inspecting repairs'. Banks had an early interest in botany, his researches enabling him to be elected a Fellow of the Royal Society by the age of twenty three. In 1768, in company with James Roberts of Mareham-le-Fen and Peter Briscoe, also of Revesby, he sailed under Lieutenant James Cook RN in *HMS Endeavour* to

9. Sir Joseph Banks as a young man.

explore the coasts of Australia (or 'New Holland' as it was then known). First they charted the coasts of New Zealand with such accuracy that the charts have only recently been updated. Then, in April 1770, they landed at a point named, due to Banks' efforts, 'Botany Bay'. Whilst Cook hoisted a Union Flag and claimed the land on behalf of George III, Banks explored inland coming back with numerous plant specimens — and kangaroos. On his return Banks sent the plant specimens to Kew's Royal Botanical Gardens where many were categorised under the scientific name of 'Banksia' in his honour. The kangaroos were given a home on his Revesby estates. He never sailed on another south-bound expedition but did visit Iceland in 1772. There had been plans for a further voyage to the south with Cook but Banks' plans to add to the superstructure of the *Endeavour* were flatly refused by Cook on the grounds of sea-safety and the scheme was abandoned. (Joseph Gilbert, an astronomer from Wrangle, and Robert Rollet of Boston did, however, sail with Cook on his second voyage.) Banks, nevertheless, maintained an interest in Cook's second and third voyages of exploration and, when, in 1787, he put forward a scheme for transporting bread-fruit from the Pacific islands to the West Indies, he suggested that the sailing-master from Cook's third voyage, one William Bligh – by now promoted to lieutenant – be given command. To boost the prestige of the expedition he strongly urged that Bligh be promoted captain for the voyage, a promotion that would have entitled Bligh to have a commissioned officer as his second-in-command, and his ship, *HMS Bounty*, to have carried marines. But the promotion was not forthcoming, with the consequence that a mentally unstable master's mate named Fletcher Christian put both the *Bounty* and Lieutenant Bligh on the map of naval history in a most unwelcome manner. Banks, meanwhile, had by now been elected President of the Royal Society in 1778 and knighted by his friend George III three years later. He was to live for almost another forty years and died in 1820. In Revesby church his personal banner – black with a gold cross and with gold fleurs-de-lys in each quarter, fringed with gold and carrying the words 'Sir Joseph Banks Bart' – hangs close to his great-grandfather's tomb.

10. Sir Joseph Banks in later years.
From an engraving by C. E. Wagstaff of a painting by T. Phillips
in the possession of The Royal Society.

Lincolnshire's connection with the Bounty mutiny was not to end with Bank's attempt to obtain promotion for Lieutenant Bligh. Edward Edwards was born at Water Newton – six miles south of Stamford – in 1741. Fourteen years later he entered the Royal Navy as a Midshipman (his rank suggesting knowledge of someone with 'interest'). By the time he was eighteen he was successful in passing his Lieutenant's examination and – despite his youth – gaining an immediate appointment in that rank. It was to be twenty-one years before his next promotion during which time he saw considerable action during the American War of Independence and service in nine ships, two of which he was appointed to command – the 'bomb' *Carcass* (later used for Arctic exploration with a Midshipman Horatio Nelson as one of the ship's company) and the sloop *Hornet*.

Edwards' first appointment as a captain was the sixth rate, twenty-gun, *Narcissus*. Whilst the ship cruised off the coast of North America one of the ship's company was disturbed from sleep by unusual sounds coming from the deck below. The seaman reported his concern to the Officer of the Watch who, in turn, informed Captain Edwards. The captain immediately 'cleared lower deck' (ie ordered all hands up from below) only to discover that at least fifty of his men had planned to take over his ship and hand it over to the rebellious colonists. After a Court Martial six of the mutineers were hanged from the *Narcissus's* yard-arm whilst others were flogged for their involvement.

Upon eventually being relieved of his command Captain Edwards was placed on half-pay, setting up house and home in Stamford. After a few years of inactivity he received, in 1790, an appointment to comand *HMS Pandora*, a 6th rate frigate, carrying twenty-four guns and a ship's company of 160 officers and men, currently fitting out at Chatham. Now being in a position of 'interest' in his own right Edwards took with him the son of a neighbour, the fifteen years old David Renouard. The young man suffered from a speech defect and had originally been accepted by Edwards as a clerk but was later 'rated' as a midshipman.

It can only be guessed at what Edwards' feelings were when he learned of the role the *Pandora* had been selected to play. Intelligence had been received by the Admiralty that some of the *Bounty* mutineers were living on the island of Otaheite (Tahiti) and the *Pandora* was to sail into the Pacific to capture them and bring them home to face justice. Such a task must have been extremely welcome to a captain who had narrowly missed being caught out by his own mutineers – possibly resulting in his having to spend such a long time ashore on half-pay. Having succeded in putting down his own mutiny he now found himself with the opportunity, and responsibility, of further pressing home the message that the Royal Navy would not tolerate such insurrections. Amongst his officers on the *Pandora* was Lieutenant Hayward who, as a midshipman, had been on the *Bounty* at the time of the mutiny and had been cast adrift in an open boat along with Bligh.

The *Pandora* sailed at the end of 1790 and reached her destination in the March of the following year. Although the mutineers had enjoyed the 'courteous manners of the natives and, above all, the blandishments of the females' they had managed to quarrel between themselves and most seemed resigned to giving themselves up to Edwards. Saddest of all was a young midshipman from the *Bounty* who had been swept along with the mutineers.

He had married the daughter of one of the local chiefs and, when he was placed in a cage built under Edwards' orders on the upper deck ('Pandora's Box'), the woman, clutching a small child paddled out to the ship. Once on board she began to weep and wail in such a forlorn manner that the midshipman begged that she be taken from the vessel and never allowed on board to see him in that condition again. The woman distressed everyone in sight by struggling violently against being removed from the ship. Eventually, she was forced back to the beach where she remained pining for her lover. She died of a broken heart shortly afterwards.

Not all the mutineers had given themselves up easily and some had tried to escape to sea before being captured. Their vessel was a small schooner they had built during their time on the island and Edwards commandeered the vessel to act as tender to his ship. The captain then had the idea that he should cruise around the nearby islands in case any of the remaining mutineers had taken refuge on them. To assist him in this plan he decided that the schooner should also patrol among the islands meeting up with him at pre-arranged rendez-vous. To command the schooner he selected Midshipman Renouard – now sixteen years old. A master's mate would help the young man with navigation and seven seamen would provide his tiny ship's company. In the beginning all went well with the schooner finding evidence of the mutineers having visited one of Palmerstone's Islands. At this information Edwards sent the tiny vessel off once again – but this time Midshipman Renouard and his command failed to return.

Captain Edwards searched the area for a month in an effort to find the schooner but all to no avail. Eventually, he was forced to the conclusion that the vessel and its crew were lost and *Pandora* headed westward with its forlorn cargo of fourteen mutineers caged inside 'Pandora's Box'.

As part of his original instructions Edwards was to investigate the possibility of a new route through the Endeavour Strait separating the north-east corner of Australia from New Guinea. Consequently, on the 28 August 1791, the *Pandora* found herself just south of the strait but with her passage barred by the Great Barrier Reef. Edwards sent out a boat to try and locate a gap through which he could take his ship and, after three hours of cautiously feeling their way down the fearsome obstacle, the boat signalled back that an opening had been found. Just as the ship reached the boat's position a large wave lifted the *Pandora* and brought her stern crashing down onto the reef wrenching off the rudder and smashing the sternpost. Within minutes the Captain was told that there were eighteen inches of water in the hold. After a quarter of an hour this had increased to nine feet. To make matters worse the weather began to deteriorate rapidly and wave after wave caused the ship to pound repeatedly against the rocks, each collision threatening to rip out the ship's bottom. Edwards gave orders that the pumps must be manned continuously, even releasing three of his prisoners to lend a hand. After two and a half hours the *Pandora* beat her way over the reef and settled into calmer waters on the other side. But there was no time to rest and throughout the night the pumps were kept going in an effort to reduce the water in the ship's hold. After dropping an anchor Edwards ordered that a sail be dragged under the ship in an attempt to block the holes in the ship's bottom but, as this was being done, one of the two pumps broke down and the sail had to be abandoned in order that the men employed on its preparation could be used to throw overboard the ship's guns. As this was being done the ship suddenly heeled over, the loosened guns running over the decks and crushing one man to death. Another died when a spare topmast fell from its fitting. The Captain, after consulting the other officers, (and getting the ship's surgeon to sign a statement on the back of a blank stores list to the effect that the ship could not be saved) decided that the vessel should be abandoned and ordered everything that could float to be thrown overboard. At this point Edwards then gave some thought to the remaining prisoners. Just as he was ordering their release an officer shouted that the bows had now gone under and water was pouring into the ship. At this the officer leaped over the side – followed immediately by the Captain. A brave attempt was made by some of the ship's company to rescue the manacled prisoners but four were still trapped as the ship plunged fifteen fathoms before settling herself upright on the bottom, her mast stumps remaining clear of the water.

Many of the survivors, clutching at spars, booms, and hen-coops, made their way towards a sand-bank some three miles from the wreck. Others swam to the ship's boats and then made their way to the same destination. When a muster was held it was found that thirty-five of the ship's company had been lost and ten of the prisoners had come through the ordeal. Although life for all involved was clearly going to be less than comfortable for some time the unfortunate prisoners were placed in the charge of Lieutenant Hayward who looked as if he was going to endure a second long open boat journey thanks to these men. Despite having spent much of the last five months in irons and confined in 'Pandora's Box' Hayward refused the prisoners any shelter from the burning heat – an act of unnecessary harshness that was later to reflect upon his Captain.

The following two days were spent in preparing the four surviving ship's boats for a journey northwards towards the Dutch controlled island of Timor. The supplies that had been recovered from the *Pandora* consisted only of a small barrel of water, a keg of wine, and a few ship's biscuits. It was calculated that, with the water in such short supply, each man would have to survive for eight days on the equivalent of a daily ration of a small wine-glass full. Even at that rate of rationing the entire supply would be gone in sixteen days. The biscuits were to be rationed out at the rate of one musket ball's weight per man per day.

The four boats set sail from the sand-bank on 31 August and embarked upon a voyage that was marked by extreme suffering by all involved. Attempts to land on any of the islands they passed were thwarted by hostile natives and attempts to protect themselves from the sun by wetting their clothing caused the salt to be absorbed through their skin. This made their saliva take on a salty taste that further added to their torment and made their efforts to eat their meagre rations difficult in the extreme. Not surprisingly, they became 'more cross and savage in temper'.

Their suffering, however, was to be rewarded. After sixteen days, and a voyage of 1,120 miles the keels of their boats grounded on the island of Timor where friendly natives looked after their immediate needs. Following a day's rest Edwards set out along the coast towards the Dutch settlement of Kupang. Here they received a warm welcome and, after a rest lasting five weeks, the *Pandora's* survivors boarded a Dutch East India vessel headed for Batavia (now Jakarta). As they sailed past the island of Flores a violent storm overtook their ship. Within minutes every sail was torn to shreds, the hold began to fill with water, and the pumps became choked. As the situation grew ever more perilous with the ship drifting rapidly towards the shore the Dutch crew 'shrunk below' leaving the vessel at the mercy of the elements. At this Captain Edwards took charge and ordered his men to take the place of the ship's crew. The *Pandora's* men then 'by manly exertion preserved the ship'. When the storm subsided it was decided to call into the small port of Semarang on Java to effect repairs. As they limped into the harbour their surprise and delight may be imagined when they spotted, tied up alongside the harbour wall, the tiny schooner that had disappeared months ago in the Samoan Islands. They were to learn from its youthful commander that when they had separated from the *Pandora* over five months earlier they had come under attack by hostile natives and had come close to losing both their ship and their lives. Having repulsed this assault, and whilst searching for the *Pandora*, they had come under attack yet again. The natural caution this state of affairs had promoted kept the small vessel clear of other islands and caused them to miss their rendezvous with the *Pandora*. After some weeks cruising the area in the hope of finding their mother ship Midshipman Renouard decided to head westwards in the hope of reaching Timor. By the time they reached the Endeavour Straits they were desperately short of water and were only saved by a lucky encounter with a Dutch ship which gave them supplies. Passing safely through the Barrier Reef they pressed on towards Timor where they took on supplies prior to continuing their westward voyage to their chance meeting with Captain Edwards and the other survivors. The young midshipman had sailed five thousand miles to reach the coast of Java.

With both groups safely at Batavia Edwards arranged passage for his men to the Cape of Good Hope where they joined *HMS Gorgon* for passage home arriving at Portsmouth on 19 June 1792.

On the 10 September that year, almost exactly a year after he had reached Timor, Captain Edwards faced a court-martial to answer for the loss of his ship. After all the officers involved had been heard the court came to the conclusions that Edwards was without blame. Nevertheless, he was never again to be given the command of a ship. His next appointment was as a 'regulating' (ie recruiting) captain in Scotland followed by a similar job in Hull. He was promoted Rear-Admiral in 1801 and received an invitation to Nelson's funeral four years later — the service for which was conducted by the Bishop of

Lincoln. By the time of his promotion to Vice-Admiral in 1808 Edwards was once again settled in Stamford. In 1810, at the age of sixty-nine, his promotion to Admiral was announced. He died four years later and was buried in the church at Water Newton in which he had been baptised.

Although clearly demonstrating the kind of leadership always welcome in the Royal Navy, Midshipman Renouard seems to have thought again about his career. As no record exists of his attempting the Lieutenant's examination, and as his name does not appear in any subsequent Navy Lists, it has to be assumed that he chose a perhaps less demanding pattern to his life (his father had been the Adjutant of the Rutlandshire Militia).

Before he died Sir Joseph Banks gave his support to a second bread-fruit expedition led by Bligh and was almost certainly instrumental in recommending a young midshipman, Matthew Flinders, for an appointment to the ship. Flinders, who was born at Donington, near Boston, in 1774, came from a family of surgeons and claimed to have obtained his love of the sea from reading 'Robinson Crusoe'. After his service under Bligh he was appointed as a midshipman on board *HMS Bellerophon* ('Billy Ruffian' to her ship's company) where he saw action in the battle of 'The Glorious First of June' – so named because of the lack of nearby land after which to name the battle. During the battle the fourteen years old Flinders came close to putting a rapid end to any future he had in the Royal Navy. As the *Bellerophon* (carrying the flag of Rear-Admiral Pasley) followed Lord Howe's flagship in breaking through the French line the captain decided to trim his sails in order to meet the threat of three French ships that he was shortly to come into close contact with. Ordering the gunners on the quarter-deck to leave their loaded cannons and to go aloft he watched as the men raced up the ratlines to carry out his commands. Suddenly Flinders, realising that a French ship was just about to pass under the quarter-deck snatched up a lighted match and, running along the entire line of cannons, fired each one in turn. No doubt pleased with himself over his actions he must have been stunned to be grabbed roughly by the collar by no less a person than Rear-Admiral Pasley himself. The admiral, white with rage, shook the midshipman violently whilst shouting over the roar of cannon, 'How dare you do this, youngster, without my orders!' Flinders, reeling from the assault, stuttered out, 'I don't know, Sir, but I thought it a fine chance to have a good shot at 'em.' His answer must have received Pasley's grudging approval for the admiral simply dropped the young midshipman from his grasp and strode off to return to the battle – the subject was never raised again. Flinders was next appointed to *HMS Reliance* where he met George Bass, a naval surgeon originally from Aswarby near Sleaford, but now with his home in Boston. Both men had a keen interest in exploration and spent considerable time away from their ship examining the coast of south-east Australia and sailing round Van Diemen's Land (later known as Tasmania). Their voyage together through the straits separating Tasmania from the mainland of Australia resulted in Flinders later naming this stretch of water 'Bass Strait' in honour of his friend. Bass also took a great interest in the flora and fauna of the new continent, becoming the first expert on the wombat and sending plant specimens home to Banks. He was to be lost at sea, somewhere in the South Pacific, in 1803 – a plaque in Boston church reminding succeeding generations of his 'gallant part in the explorations of Australia'.

Flinders, meanwhile, returned to Lincolnshire to marry Anne Chappell at Partney church in 1800. His new wife was the step-daughter of the recently deceased rector of Bratoft, the Reverend William Tyler. Her father had died at sea in command of a Baltic trader out of Hull. During his time in the county he paid a call on Sir Joseph Banks at Revesby and pursuaded him of the importance of further exploration of the Australian coast. Banks, easily fired by such suggestions, in turn gained Admiralty approval for such an expedition and, in January 1801, Flinders – now promoted to commander – set sail for

11. Captain Matthew Flinders, R. N.
From a painting by T. A. de Chazal in Mauritius.

Australia in command of *HMS Investigator*. With him he took his brother, Lieutenant Samuel Flinders, and a young cousin, Midshipman John Franklin of Spilsby. His first-lieutenant was Robert Fowler of Horncastle who was later to reach the rank of vice-admiral.

The voyage of the *Investigator* was a triumph of navigation and exploration – assisted, no doubt, by Flinder's practice of placing a small iron bar by his ship's compass to compensate for the magnetic deviation caused through large iron objects in the ship itself. The 'Flinders' Bar' rapidly became a standard item of navigational equipment in all ships at sea. Exploring the South Australia coast Flinders, in addition to naming Bass Straits, also named Cape Donington, Spalding Cove, Sleaford Bay, Revesby Island, Sir Joseph Banks Islands, Port Lincoln and many other places in recognition of his county and of the friends who had aided him in his explorations. Eventually he was completely to circumnavigate the continent proving beyond doubt that it was a land mass rather than a group of islands.

Until this time, what had been known of the continent, had been named New Holland. Flinders renamed it 'Terra Australis'. This caused a correspondent to the 'Naval Chronicle' to write 'we do not altogether approve of the needless recourse to a dead language. Why not call it more concisely *Australia?*'

Leaving *HMS Investigator* on station in 1803 – 'not worth repairing' and consequently converted into a storage hulk – he, along with some of his officers and ship's company, took passage in *HMS Porpoise,* in company with *HMS*

12. The wrecking of the Porpoise and Cato.
From *The Mariner's Chronicle*, 1805, p. 385.

Cato, in order to get his information back to England as quickly as possible with a request for another vessel to complete the exploration. Six days out of Sidney the *Porpoise* and *Cato* both struck a reef. After struggling onto a sandbank the shipwrecked men took stock of their situation. They were 200 miles from land and 750 miles from Port Jackson, the nearest settlement. It was decided that Flinders would take one of the ship's six-oared cutters and try to reach help. After a long and anxious wait of over six weeks the sails of *HMS Rollo* appeared over the horizon with Flinders at the helm. Once his ship's company had been put aboard the *Rollo* Flinders transferred to *HMS Cumberland*, a fast schooner, for the voyage home to England. But still his luck held against him. Unaware that England was now at war with France the ship called into Mauritius where, '. . . shocking to relate, instead of being received with kindness, as is the practice of civilised nations to nautical discoverers, he was put in prison by the governor, De-Caen, and confined for six years and a half.' He was released in 1810. With his health broken he was unable to resume his naval career despite being promoted to captain in May 1810. Turning to writing an account of his voyages he was to die in July 1814 just before his work was to be published. Sadly, the whereabouts of his burial place has been lost (it was probably in Woolwich) but Donington church holds a bronze bust of Flinders and a plaque records that: 'His country will long regret the loss of one whose exertions in her cause were only equalled by his perseverence'. The Seamen's chapel in Lincoln Cathedral holds a splendid model of *HMS Investigator*. His grandson was the famous Egyptologist, William Matthew Flinders Petrie.

Close by Matthew's memorial is another to his brother, 'Samuel Ward Flinders, Lieutenant of the Royal Navy', who died in 1834, aged fifty-two.

13. A model of HMS Investigator in The Seaman's Chapel in Lincoln Cathedral.

Unfortunately his career was not as distinguished as his elder brother with naval records showing him to be one of a very rare group of individuals who have two seniority dates for their promotion to lieutenant. Having first been promoted on 3 March 1801 a subsequent court martial 'reduced' him to a new date exactly three years later.

Not everyone can blaze their name into the highest reaches of the Royal Navy, despite long and loyal service. The Honourable Thomas Shirley, the fifth son of the sixth Earl of Ferrers passed his lieutenant's examination on the 11 October 1755. In less than three years he had been promoted to commander and nine months later to captain. Such rapid promotion was not unusual during war time when the casualty rate amongst senior officers could be very high. His first command (9 November 1759) was *HMS Garland*, followed shortly afterwards by a re-appointment to the sixty-gun *Kingston*. Two years later he transferred to *HMS Princess Mary* where he remained until the end of the Seven Years War.

With the war over, Captain Shirley found himself without a ship and on half-pay. He did, however, manage to boost his income by obtaining an appointment as Deputy-Ranger of London's royal parks.

In July 1780 he was appointed to *HMS Leander*, a newly launched ship of fifty guns. One of Shirley's first responsibilities was to find himself a ship's company. Although he would have had a press gang ashore on the look-out for seamen he, like other captains, cruised the North Sea and English Channel hoping to come across a merchantman from whom he could press valuable trained men. At the beginning of November just such a vessel was spotted

14. HMS Union — Captain Shirley's last command

heading in their direction. Knowing full well what was likely to happen the merchant ship, ignoring Shirley's signals ordering her to hove to, crammed on full sail in an effort to outrun the warship. Shirley, no doubt fuming at this slight to his authority, ordered a cannon-ball to be fired across her bows. Much to his mortification, he quickly discovered that the gunpowder with which he had been supplied proved to be of such poor quality that the projectile struggled to reach the end of the cannon and fell harmlessly into the sea well short of its target. To his further fury, the merchantman surged past the *Leander* with the roars of laughter and cat-calls of her crew echoing around his ears.

Having eventually acquired a full complement, *Leander* was ordered to the west coast of Africa where Captain Shirley distinguished himself by capturing five Dutch forts along with 124 guns. He also destroyed a French store-ship valued at £30,000.

Sent with his ship to the West Indies station in 1782, Shirley found himself re-appointed to the command of *HMS Union*, a splendid second rate of ninety guns. He brought his ship home to England during the following summer where the cessation of hostilities saw his ship taken out of commission and himself put ashore. With the war over, and few opportunities for employment at sea, most captains found themselves ashore on half-pay. The problem was made much worse by the fact that with the promotion to flag rank (i.e. rear-admirals and above) being based on the roster system, and with so many captains on the waiting list, promotion could be a very long way off indeed. Over thirty-one years after his promotion to captain, the Honourable Thomas Shirley was still waiting for his turn to come up. In an effort to clear this logjam the Admiralty introduced the 'superannuated rear-admiral' scheme under which senior captains could take promotion to rear-admiral and promptly retire with a pension of 17/6d per day. Known in the Navy as 'rear-admirals of the yellow' (as opposed to the 'red', 'white' or 'blue' squadrons) many took this handsome and honourable way out of stagnation. Amongst those 'Yellowed' was Thomas Shirley who went on to live to the age of eighty-one, building and living in Horkstow Hall before dying 'sincerely lamented' in 1814. He is buried in St. Maurice's church, Horkstow — some three miles from Barton-upon-Humber.

Another naval officer to follow a similar path was Thomas Steventon. However, for him there was not the glory of early promotion. Instead, Steventon was thirty two years old before he passed his lieutenant's examination — indicating, perhaps, either long service on the 'lower deck' as a seaman prior to taking the examination (extremely rare) or, a certain slowness in learning his professional skills as a midshipman or master's mate. Whatever the reason, thirty-one years after his promotion Steventon was still a lieutenant, having spent the vast majority of his service to the Crown ashore on half-pay (three shillings per day). By that time, 1831, the Royal Navy had over 4,000 lieutenants on the Navy List with jobs for only a fraction of them. The time had come to clear away the 'dead wood'. A few lucky lieutenants were made 'superannuated commanders' and retired with a commander's pension, others — Steventon (now aged sixty-three) amongst them — kept their half-pay and were promoted to 'retired commander' but with no further chance of sea-time or prospects of promotion. Effectively they were dismissed the Service on the day of their promotion.

Thomas Steventon died six years after his naval career came to an end. He is buried in the grounds of Kingerby church with the words 'Commander in the Royal Navy' proudly carved into his tombstone.

The Cox family of Lincolnshire had a long tradition of military service to the country — one of their number even reaching the height of commanding the Second Battalion of the Lincolnshire Regiment during the First World War. One of his ancesters, however, Douglas Cox — despite being the son of an army officer — opted for a career at sea. In May, 1800, at the age of eleven the young Cox entered the Service on board the thirty-two-gun *Boston* as a first class volunteer and spent the next four years in blockading duties off the coast of North America. He then moved onto the *Circe* and served in the West Indies where his ship did valuable work in capturing or destroying French and Spanish privateers. After eighteen months of this work he was transferred to the flagship of Rear-Admiral The Honourable Sir Alexander Cochrane, *HMS Northumberland*. Cox (by now almost certainly a midshipman) clearly made a good impression for, after only eight months, he was appointed sub-lieutenant on the gun-brig, *HMS Attentive*. The rank of sub-lieutenant had been created by Admiral The Earl St Vincent as a means of promoting deserving young midshipmen who had 'passed for' lieutenant but for whom no vacancy for a commission could be found (the rank was replaced after only a few years by the rank of 'mate' and did not re-appear until 1861).

His elevation in rank seems to have been well justified as his conduct in action was soon to show. Given the job of 'cutting out' a Spanish coastguard vessel (i.e. capturing it from inside an enemy harbour) he approached the ship in a small boat manned only by himself and five seamen. As he drew near the alarm was given on the Spaniard and the thirty-five man crew turned out on the upper deck fully armed to meet the threat. Not bothering to load the ship's two six-pounder cannons the Spanish were content to wait for Cox's party with their swords and muskets. Their mistake quickly became evident when Cox, leaping over the enemy gunwhale, led his small band in a furious attack against the coastguard ship's crew. Within minutes the Spanish had surrend- ered and the ship was in Cox's hands. He was seventeen years old at the time.

At the end of 1807 Cox was sent first to the *Port D'Espagne* with the rank of acting-lieutenant and then on to the sixteen-gun *HMS Snap* where, two weeks after taking part in the capture of Martinique, he was finally confirmed in the rank of lieutenant in March 1809. Two years later, as first lieutenant of the *Snap*, he was responsible for bringing the ship successfully into action against a much larger vessel under the heavy guns of enemy batteries firing from the shore. He then went ashore himself and served alongside the soldiers in the taking of Guadeloupe, an enemy base in the Windward Islands.

For the next ten years Lieutenant Cox served on a variety of ships visiting the Mediterranean, the East Indies and China, before returning to the West Indies where, at long last, he received his own command (still as a lieutenant), the tiny sloop *Shearwater*. After only eighteen months he was ordered to bring her back to England where she was 'paid off' and he was put ashore on half pay – the fate of many officers now that there was no war for them to fight.

After twelve years ashore Cox managed to find a job as Inspector of Coastguards which lasted for no more than two-and-a-half years. Despite the continued time on half pay he was promoted to captain in November 1841 and placed on the Retired List in June 1854. Until that date, and regardless of a brilliant start to his careers, Douglas Cox had spent 24 years on active service with the Royal Navy, and 35 years on half pay. But his career had not quite ended. For

15. Rear-Admiral Cox's Naval General Service Medal. Now in The Museum of Lincolnshire Life, Burton Road, Lincoln.

some reason — probably the outbreak of the Crimean War — his name was taken off the Retired List and placed once more on the Active List. Although he did not see any further active service he was fortunate enough whilst on the Active List to have built up enough seniority to be promoted to Rear-Admiral two years before his death in February 1863.

Douglas Cox's Naval General Service medal with the 'Martinique' and 'Guadeloupe' clasps can be found in the Museum of Lincolnshire Life, the sole naval award amongst the military distinctions won by his shore-serving relations.

The Naval General Service medal won by Cox was the 1848 issue that covered the years 1793-1840. There were 230 different clasps (bars) that could be awarded with the medal ranging from major battles such as Camperdown and Trafalgar to small 'cutting out' expeditions. The youngest person to win the medal was less than one day old — having been born just before the battle of the Glorious First of June 1794 (his mother was refused the medal by the Admiralty because she was a woman).

PRESS GANGS AT LARGE

ALMOST TO A MAN, officers in the Royal Navy had volunteered to serve their country at sea. The Marines ('Royal' from 1802) also had no difficulty in recruiting their men and Lincolnshire must have been seen as a potentially good place to seek new men for the Corps when *a Rendezvous* (recruiting station) was set up at The Globe, Waterside, Lincoln in 1790. The same eagerness to serve could not, however, be said of many of the seamen who served with them. Of course, many men did volunteer, but, in time of war, there were never enough to man Britain's warships. When this happened, the press gang took to the streets and public houses of ports and harbours in an effort to swell the numbers of seamen available to the Navy. After some centuries of haphazard organisation the Royal Navy, in 1792, formalised the system under the 'Impressment Service'. In January the following year Lieutenant Edmund Elliston set up his *Rendezvous* at The Golden Fleece in Gainsborough. In the beginning all seemed well as the following month the local 'Committee for Managing the Subscription' lent their support by offering a bounty to all who volunteered and were 'approved' by Lieutenant Elliston. But, by May, events took a serious turn when 'a riot of a very alarming nature' broke out. Seamen 'armed with bludgeons and pistols, and heated with liquor' attacked Elliston after a seaman named Hall 'an obnoxious character' had been taken by the press gang. The officer was knocked to the ground and, with his sword broken, would 'in all probability have been murdered' had it not been for the intervention of bystanders.

Such an uproar does not appear to have deterred Elliston for four years later he was still in the town when a forty-three years old seaman died after swimming the River Trent in an effort to escape his press gang. Forty-nine years later the local press reported the death of Robert Wright aged eighty-two, 'the last of the Gainsborough Press Gang'.

Gainsborough was not the only place to suffer from the presence of the press gang. The nation's fishing fleets had for many years been considered as 'the nursery of the Navy' and had voluntarily provided many prime seamen who wished to serve on a royal ship. As a result it had become established practise that fishermen were not pressed. But, with the country under serious threat of invasion in 1805 (the year of Trafalgar), the Impress Service was told to institute a 'hot press' – anybody who looked like a seaman could be taken. As a result, when the fishermen of Grimsby returned from the 'Great Fishery' on the Dogger Bank, they found themselves confronted by sleek, fast, press tenders which came alongside, boarded, and helped themselves to the best of the fishermen. So many men were taken that the press tender's holds were full to overflowing and a few lucky fishermen found themselves returned to their boats and, ultimately, their families.

FRANKLIN AND THE NORTH-WEST PASSAGE

There was no risk of young Spilsby-born John Franklin being forcibly pressed into the Royal Navy. Despite opposition from his father (who thought that sailors were a 'careless, swearing, reprobate, and good-for-nothing set of men') he managed to have himself appointed to *HMS Polyphemus* as a first class volunteer. Although delighted with his good fortune, he wrote to his father to see if any influence could be used to have him re-appointed to *HMS Investigator* under the command of his cousin, Commander Matthew Flinders, as he had heard that the *Investigator* was to explore the coasts of Australia. But, before any influence could be brought to bear, *Polyphemus* had sailed for the Baltic to join the flag of Admiral Sir Hyde Parker. Eighteen days later Franklin found himself sailing with the squadron led by Parker's Second-in-Command, Lord Nelson, to a position 200 yards from the Danish fleet. As the line was established eight hundred Danish guns roared out against seven hundred English. For over four hours the two fleets hammered at each other without moving, *Polyphemus* being in the unfortunate position of having the fire of two Danish ships poured down upon her whilst Nelson was putting his telescope to his blind eye ('Leave off action! Now damn me if I do!'). Eventually, the firing from the Danes fell away and *Polyphemus* took possession of the two ships opposing her. Franklin looked over the side of his ship and 'saw a prodigious number of the slain at the bottom of the remarkably clear water'. He was fourteen years old.

Having survived the Battle of Copenhagen his luck continued when three months later he joined his cousin on board the *Investigator* where he was promoted to midshipman. He learned well under Flinders and earned his respect. ('He is a very fine youth' Flinders wrote to his parents.) After being stranded for six weeks on a sand bank following the wreck of the *Porpoise*, (see pages 28-29) Franklin was put aboard the *Rollo* which sailed for Canton. When he arrived he found sixteen ships of the East India Company just about to sail for England so he secured himself a job as signal midshipman on the *Earl of*

16. Franklin, as a young man, depicted holding a broken spar and standing on the reef following the wrecking of the 'Porpoise'.

Camden – the flagship. As the merchantmen entered the Straits of Malacca they ran into a heavily armed Fench squadron which included an eighty-four gun line-of-battle ship. The French, expecting an easy victory, were stunned when, acting upon the orders of his commodore, Franklin ran up the signal 'tack in succession, bear down in line ahead, and engage the enemy'. After a sharp engagement lasting three quarters of an hour the enemy withdrew and Franklin was ordered to make the signal for 'general chase'. The French fled.

Upon his arrival in England Franklin was given six weeks leave before being appointed to *HMS Bellerophon* (Flinders' old ship). The early part of 1805 was spent in blockading duties off Brest before joining Admiral Collingwood's ships off Cadiz. In September Nelson arrived in the *Victory* and, on the 21st of the following month, the *Bellerophon* found herself as the sixth ship in Collingwood's division as they bore down on a long line of French and Spanish ships off Cape Trafalgar.

As Franklin took his position as signal midshipman on the poop deck the men on the gun-decks chalked 'Victory or Death' along the barrels of their cannons. Twenty minutes after Collingwood had breached the enemy line the *Bellerophon* came up to the action and found herself under fire from two ships at the same time. The situation rapidly worsened as her rigging became tangled up with the rigging of the Frenchman *L'Aigle*. Four other ships now joined in to pour their fire into *Bellerophon* whilst *L'Aigle* swept her decks with musket fire and grenades. Of the forty-seven men stationed on the English ship's poop and quarter decks forty were killed or wounded (including the captain who, like Nelson, had insisted on wearing his best uniform into battle). Twice the enemy tried to board from *L'Aigle* but were forced back by the English swarming up from below decks. Franklin later wrote: 'In this way hundreds of them fell between the ships and were drowned.' He had passed through the worst of the firing and had come out of it unscathed (apart from a slight deafness – as a result of the intense cannon fire – which was to remain with him for the remainder of his life) and, when not repelling boarders, busied himself among the wounded, there being no opportunities for signal flying whilst locked against the enemy. Eventually the fire from *L'Aigle's* cannon died away and the English gunners on the lower gundecks angled their cannon upwards so that their shot smashed through the enemy decks. At that moment the ships wrenched apart and *L'Aigle* drifted away, unable to reply to the continued English assault and, shortly afterwards, struck her colours to *HMS Defiance*. The *Bellerophon* settled for the capture of two of the other ships that had fought against her in the battle.

After a further two years on the *Bellerophon* Franklin transferred to *HMS Bedford* as master's mate. Before 1807 was out he had passed his lieutentant's examination but remained on the *Bedford* for the next seven years. During this time he saw action in the American War of 1812, being wounded in the attack on New Orleans. In July 1815 he joined *HMS Forth* as first (i.e. senior) lieutenant but, with the war against the French over, there was to be a drastic reduction of the British fleet and, in September, Franklin found himself ashore on half pay.

In 1818 the Admiralty declared itself to be back in the business of exploration by sending Captain Ross and Lieutenant Parry to try and reach the North Pole. Captain Buchan was ordered to the same destination by a different route with the additional orders that he was to attempt to find a North-West Passage connecting the Atlantic and Pacific Oceans. He was to be escorted by *HMS Trent*, commanded by Lieutenant Franklin.

The expedition was not a success mainly due to the poor quality of the vessels employed. Both ships spent time stuck in the ice pack and, with timbers weakened beyond recovery, had to return. The following year Parry was again sent north, this time to Baffin's Bay, and Franklin was given command of a west to east overland party that was to link up with the ships. Again Franklin failed to reach his goal but, this time, it was the weather conditions combined with native treachery that caused his failure. Indeed, it was Franklin's refusal to give way to despair (despite having to resort to surviving on lichen and old shoe leather) that had brought out the survivors and, in recognition of this, he was promoted captain and elected a Fellow of the Royal Society.

'The man who ate his boots' married Eleanor Anne Porden in 1823.

By any standards Eleanor was a remarkable woman. She had been attending Royal Society lectures from the age of nine and had published a scientific poem *The Veils* at the age of sixteen. So impressive had this work been that she was elected as the first woman member of the French Institute. Encouraged by his wife, Franklin worked on the planning of a new Arctic expedition until she fell desperately ill with tuberculosis. Rather than have him delay on her account she urged him to leave on the day planned and he, reluctantly, agreed. Eleanor died six days after he had sailed.

Franklin returned to England in 1827 and re-married the following year. His new wife, Jane, was an old friend of Eleanor's and was another well educated woman with a mind of her own. Even before their marriage she had pursuaded Franklin to visit Russia to discuss Arctic exploration with the Empress and the future Czar Alexander II. Their honeymoon was spent in Paris where local Society, expecting to meet a gaunt survivor of an Arctic expedition who had been reduced to eating his boots, were stunned to find a powerfully built man weighing fifteen stone. After being knighted in 1829 for his services to exploration he was appointed to command *HMS Rainbow* ('Franklin's Paradise' as it became known to his ship's company during an eventful three years in the Mediterranean). His career then took a complete turn of direction: Captain Sir John Franklin, Royal Navy, was appointed to be Lieutenant-Governor of Van Dieman's Land (now Tasmania). Despite their new home being based upon a convict settlement Franklin and his wife, Lady Jane, were able to institute several social changes in the seven years they held the position. They established an educational college, founded a scientific group which later developed into the Royal Society of Tasmania, and created a natural history museum at their own cost. Lady Jane became the first woman to climb the island's tallest peak, Mount Wellington. Together, Franklin and his wife completed the first west to east crossing of Tasmania, at one stage having to build a raft to get them across a flooded river that was to be named after the Lieutenant-Governor.

After his return to England in 1844 Franklin was consulted about a new Arctic expedition to find the North-West Passage and immediately offered himself as leader. Even his friends opposed the idea, one suggesting that, after all, he was fifty-nine years old. 'Not quite,' he replied – he still had three months to go before reaching that age – and, again with his wife's blessing, he managed to have himself placed in command.

This time his ships were known to be sound enough for the voyage ahead. *HMS Terror* and *HMS Erebus* carried a full suit of sails which were backed up by 50 horse-power steam engines driving screw propellors. Both ships had seen service in the Antarctic under Captain Sir James Ross who had named two volcanoes in their honour. Each ship carried 67 officers and ratings and had provisions enough to last for three years.

On 4 July 1845 the ships called at Whalefish Island, on Canada's eastern seaboard, and sailed eight days later. On 27 July they were seen by a whaling ship in Melville Bay sailing away among the icebergs. They were never seen again.

When, by 1848, it was clear that Franklin was well overdue a series of searches were mounted to try and find him and his expedition. The government offered a reward of £20,000 to which Lady Franklin added a further £3,000. The first traces were found in the summer of 1850 when a party from *HMS Assistance* found three tombstones. Four years later an overland party brought out silver-ware belonging to Franklin that had been purchased from some Eskimos. In the meantime, the Royal Navy had not given up hope, Franklin's promotion to rear-admiral was announced in October 1852.

As a last desperate measure Lady Franklin organised a private expedition, led by naval officers, which left in July 1857. Almost two years later the expedition found a note under a cairn which unravelled the mystery of Franklin's disappearance. The first part of the note was written by one of Franklin's officers who had been sent ahead, over the ice that was blocking the ship's passage, to see what lay ahead. It recorded the momentous news that the coast of North America could be seen from the hills of King William's Island. Only twelve miles of ice prevented the ships from reaching the Pacific Ocean – the North-West Passage had been discovered. The elation of this part of the note was to be dashed by script in a different hand around the edges of the paper. Sir John Franklin had died on 11 June 1847, possibly aware of his achievement. Within a year the entire party had perished. They had 'forged the last link with their lives'.

A plaque on the wall of a bakery in Spilsby's High Street marks Franklin's birthplace and a splendid bronze statue dominates the town's market place. Other statues have been erected at Waterloo Place, London, and at Hobart, the capital of Tasmania. Perhaps, however, Sir John Franklin's best epitaph comes from two Eskimoes who told one search expedition officer that they

17. The last sighting of HMS Terror and HMS Erebus.

remembered: 'An old man, with broad shoulders, grey hair, full face and bald head. He wore spectacles, was quite lame and appeared sick. But, despite his ill health, he was always laughing.'

In 1990 a Royal Navy expedition, sponsored by the people of Lincolnshire and led by the author, attempted to find the remains of Sir John Franklin. The expedition had no more success than its predecessors in locating the grave of Franklin but did find a skull on Todd Island and part of a musket carved from caribou antler on Booth Point – both places on the route used by the Ship's companies in their ill-fated attempt to reach help.†

---

† See note on page 79

SIR JOHN FRANKLIN
DISCOVERER OF THE NORTH WEST PASSAGE
BORN AT SPILSBY
APRIL 1786
DIED IN THE ARCTIC REGIONS
JUNE 1847

ERECTED BY PUBLIC SUBSCRIPTION

18. The statue erected in Spilsby Market Place
to Sir John Franklin. Spilsby's most famous son.

THE FANES OF FULBECK

THE FANE FAMILY of Fulbeck had also suffered two tragic losses during the early years of the nineteenth century. Lieutenant Neville Fane, appointed to the West Indies Station on board *HMS Blonde*, died of the yellow fever and was buried at Bridgetown, Barbados. At about the time he died his close relation, Vere Fane, was born. Nineteen years later Vere Fane was a lieutenant on the ten-gun brig *HMS Algerine* sailing off the Greek mainland in company with *HMS Cambrian* and *HMS Revenge*. Suddenly, without warning, the ships were hit by a sharp squall. *Cambrian* and *Revenge* were badly damaged but the *Algerine* rolled over and capsized with the loss of all hands. Both Neville and Vere Fane were nineteen years old when they died at a time when the minimum age for a Royal Navy lieutenant was supposed to be twenty-one. The Navy, however, accepted the practice that promising young men could pass their lieutenant's examination early. Both have memorials in Fulbeck church.

Another member of the same family, Robert, carved himself a unique place in naval history possibly without ever setting foot on board a ship. He married the daughter of Admiral Sir Eliab Harvey and, when she died, in 1838, he married the daughter of Admiral Sir Henry Blackwood. To have twice married daughters of Admirals may not be unique but the combined actions of his fathers-in-law most certainly was. Both were captains at the Battle of Trafalgar and, as Nelson bid farewell to his 'band of brothers', Blackwood implored him to transfer his flag to a frigate, or at the very least, not to wear his uniform coat with its covering of sparkling honours and awards as such an act would be sure to attract the attention of the enemy. But the Admiral brushed aside such suggestions and saw Blackwood on his way with the sombre, 'God bless you, Blackwood, I shall never speak to you again'. Tradition suggests that Blackwood then spoke to Captain Harvey of *HMS Temeraire* whose ship followed in the wake of *HMS Victory*. As the enemy ships grew ever closer Harvey used every breath of wind to overtake his Admiral and thus take the brunt of the first cannonading. His reward was to hear Nelson in person hailing him through a speaking trumpet with the rebuke, 'Captain Harvey, I'll thank you to keep your station, which is astern of *Victory*!'.

Both men had failed in their attempt to save their leader's life, but both had a daughter who married Robert Fane of Fulbeck.

The Napoleonic war had led to a further naval involvement in the county of Lincolnshire. In 1804 it was decided to establish a line of signalling stations up the east coast of England, four of which were to be in Lincolnshire, the most northerly of which was set up at 'Cleaness' (in the area of modern day

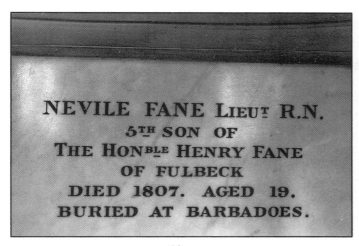

19a.

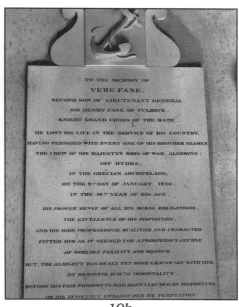

19b.

19a. and b. Fane memorials in Fulbeck Church

19c.

19d.

19c. and d. Cadet Vere William Carton Fane
Born 10th September 1892 – died 24th September 1906
(see **Page 44**)

Cleethorpes). This station received south-bound information from a station across the Humber at Dimlington and transmitted it to the next station to the south — at Saltfleet. From there it went to Sutton-on-Sea and then to Skegness. From Skegness the message was passed across the Wash to Holkham.

The stations were manned by half-pay naval lieutenants each assisted by a petty-officer or midshipman and two men — all of whom had to be 'unsuitable for ship service'. The wooden buildings, which were originally painted white but later tarred to save costs, had two rooms, one for the officer (with 'bath stove', three chairs and a table), and one for the remainder of the team who had to make do with a fire-grate and just one chair each. The officer was entitled to a 'cot' whilst the others had to 'sling' hammocks. Above them towered a thirty-foot mast with a yardarm of equal length on which to fly the signal pennants.

Whilst carrying out his duties the lieutenant earned an extra eight shillings a day on top of his half-pay (plus ninepence a mile travelling expenses): the midshipman or petty-officer earned just five shillings, and the men two. As far as is known there was no scandal to rock the Lincolnshire signal stations as happened at Portland in Dorset where the officer was found to have entered his daughter as a midshipman in order to gain access to his deputy's salary.

The Royal Navy's presence at Grimsby was highlighted in August 1808 in a most unusual manner when, over accusations of political corruption, Captain Hewson, Royal Navy, fought a duel with William Fraser — the Town Clerk. Using pistols as their weapons both missed with the first shot. Captain Hewson then demanded that the duel be continued until one of them was hit. Fraser, happy to have survived so far, refused and left the Field of Honour only to be dismissed from his office. Captain Hewson went on to marry Miss Marshall, daughter of W. Marshall Esq., of Great Grimsby.

Mid-way through the nineteenth century, with the press gang now a thing of the past, captains of ships were still required to man their own ships. One captain sent Lieutenant Butcher to open a *Rendezvous* at the Angel Inn, Boston, in February 1859. The local press reported, 'We hear that the gallant officer has been very successful'.

One young man whose station in life could have kept him well clear of common ale-houses with naval recruiting officers was the Right Honourable Lord Francis Horace Pierrepoint Cecil of Burghley House. Nevertheless, feeling the call of the sea, he entered the Navy and was promoted to midshipman in July 1866 aged fifteen. Within five years he was made a sub-lieutenant and appointed to *HMS Narcissus* — a flagship (with its consequent formality and discipline). In December 1872 he was appointed to *HMS Lord Warden,* the largest wooden ship ever built for the Royal Navy — yet another flagship (the penalty for having a noble title that could decorate the environment of a Victorian admiral). Promoted lieutenant in 1874 he found himself, almost inevitably, four years later appointed to his third flagship,

HMS Royal Adelaide, not merely as a ship's officer but as flag-lieutenant to the admiral. For a young man who may have hoped that a life at sea would have taken him from the formality of a stately home the succession of dull jobs that had come his way must have been a great disappointment. His name disappears from the Navy list in 1884. Today Lieutenant the Right Honourable Lord Francis Cecil looks down upon the diners in the Burghley House restaurant from a group portrait he shares with other members of his family.

Until 1923 the coastguard service operated under the control of the Admiralty and its ranks were filled almost exclusively with ex-Royal Navy men. Consequently, coastguard stations made excellent recruiting stations during the latter part of the nineteenth century. The station at Barrow-on-Humber was no exception and its enamel poster stating: 'Men and Boys Wanted – Good Pay & Prospects', can still be seen in Baysgarth museum,

20. Enamel recruiting poster – now in Baysgarth Museum at Barton-on-Humber.

Barton-on-Humber.

The new century had hardly got into its stride when, yet again, tragedy struck the Fulbeck Fanes. Cadet Vere Fane entered the Royal Navy at Osborne College in 1905 at the age of thirteen. He was a young man 'noble in character, gentle in disposition, and showing promise of high achievement'. The following year he collapsed and died. Such was the effect of his death upon his officers and fellow cadets that not only did the officers from Osborne

*21. Admiral The Right Hon.
Lord Charles W. D. Beresford, G.C.V.O.,
K.C.B.*

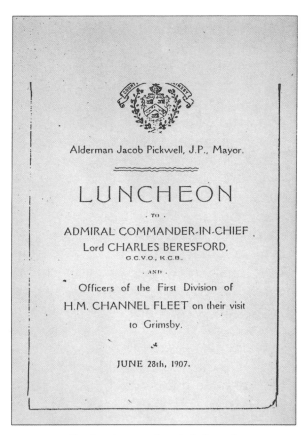

*22. Invitation to the civic luncheon
given in honour of the visit of
the First Division of the Channel Fleet,
28th June 1907.*

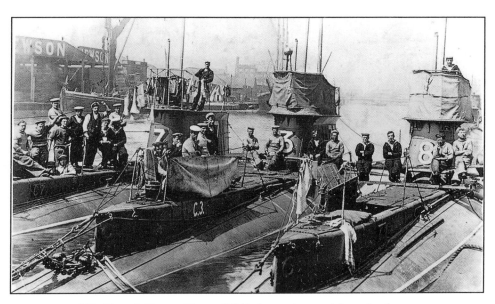

23. Royal Navy Class 'C' Submarines at Immingham.

follow his coffin through silent ranks of cadets but the captain and other officers from the Naval College at Dartmouth also attended. As a Bluejacket band from Portsmouth played the 'Dead March', the body of Vere Fane was placed on board the college torpedo boat to begin its journey home to Fulbeck with the 'Last Post' ringing out over the Solent waters. His grave (see page 42), with its cross embellished with a sculpted naval officer's cap badge, lies next to his father and close by his mother. He was their only child.

The port of Grimsby was selected for a particular honour in June 1907. The Channel Fleet's First Division, under the command of Admiral Lord Charles ('Charlie B') Beresford, paid a visit. The Mayor laid on a grand luncheon for the Commander-in-Chief and his officers whilst a programme of events was arranged for the petty officers and men. The latter included free admission to the fairground and free donkey rides.

The following year saw Grimsby hosting the sinister shapes of the Royal Navy's newly developed 'C' class submarines commanded by men like Lieutenants Nasmith and Boyle who were later to win Victoria Crosses in action against the Turks. Submarine *C2's* Grimsby visit was commanded by Lieutenant Arthur Jameson the heir to a whisky fortune. Both 'C' and 'E' Class submarines, famed equally for their prowess against the Turks, were often to be found moored alongside at Immingham.

1907 saw the establishment of a Royal Naval wireless telegraphy station at Waltham. Originally titled 'Cleethorpes' WT Station' it was the first in the country to be equipped with a high-powered transmitter and was intended for use with naval units operating in the North Sea. The aerial was raised by means of a 450-foot wooden tower which, for a time in the 1930s, became known as 'King Kong's Cigar'. During the First World War the station's most important role was the handling of the signal traffic during the Battle of Jutland in 1916. In 1934 the wooden tower burned down and was replaced by five steel pylons. With the outbreak of the Second World War the site was guarded by survivors of the 1914-1918 'Grimsby Chums' battalion who gave themselves the nickname – 'The Pyloniers'. During the war the most controversial signal to pass through the station was the order to the ships of Convoy PQ17 'convoy is to scatter'. The Admiralty believed that the *Tirpitz* was about to descend on the convoy. But the *Tirpitz* was 300 miles away in a Nowegian Fiord and the scattered, unprotected ships fell like ripe plums into the hands of waiting U-Boats and enemy aircraft. Of more than thirty ships that sailed from Iceland only eleven reached Archangel. The WT Station changed its name to 'Waltham WT Station' in 1948 and later to 'New Waltham WT Station'. It closed down in 1980 and North Lincolnshire lost one of its best known landmarks when the five pylons were demolished.

THE NAVY IN THE AIR

In 1912 CLEETHORPES was one of the landing grounds chosen by the Naval Wing of the Royal Flying Corps as part of a series of air stations stretching from North Berwick to the Lizard. However, with Admiralty oil tanks at Immingham to be defended, it was later decided that land alongside the tanks would serve as an airstrip. Originally known as *RNAS Immingham* (the Royal Naval Air Service had broken away from the Army-led Royal Flying Corps) it soon changed its name to *RNAS Killingholme* and the role of defending the oil tanks rapidly expanded into coastal patrolling. One of the earliest pilots to be sent to the airstation was Squadron-Commander Bell-Davies who bumped his way across Lincolnshire in a Sopwith Tractor biplane. After service in the Dardenelles campaign – in which he earned the Victoria Cross – Bell-Davies (now a wing-commander) came back as district commander of air stations in northern England. Under his prompting, and with the support of the Immingham-based Admiral East Coast, he expanded Killingholme's role into an anti-U-boat and anti-zeppelin base as well as a training station for sea-plane and flying-boat crews.

Among the land planes on the station were several two-seater scouts known as 'Spinning Jennys' due to their disconcerting tendency of going into a spin – usually with fatal results to the pilot. Flight-Lieutenant J. C. Brook found himself thrown into one of these deadly spins whilst operating over Killingholme. By the urgent manipulation of his controls he found, much to his surprise and, no doubt, delight, that he had regained control of the aircraft. Instead of immediately landing with the grateful knowledge that he had survived he promptly threw the aircraft into yet another – this time, deliberate – spin. By repeating the actions that had seen him safely out of the previous incident he again steadied the aircraft. Thanks to his bravery the risk to life from the aircraft's instability had been greatly reduced.

Another aircraft of particular significance at the air station was the Sopwith Schneider. Armed with a Lewis gun and a 60lb bomb they could be used against U-boats or zeppelins. With these in mind Bell-Davies, on a suggestion from his area admiral, requisitioned a Great Northern Railways paddle-steamer – appropriately named *Killingholme* – that had been used to ferry sheep across the Humber. Its wide decks could be used to carry three or four Schneiders, the aircraft to be hoisted on or off the sea by derrick. The plan was for the *Killingholme* then to sail to a position off the Dogger Bank and wait for zeppelins to appear, whereupon the aircraft would take off and bring the enemy down before they could reach the English coast. Unfortunately, the vessel had some design defects such as a compass that always pointed to the funnel regardless of the true bearing of magnetic north, a funnel that wobbled with every wave, rudders that obeyed only a will of their own, and paddles that were made deliberately fragile in case they hit the bottom of the Humber. This latter flaw proved to be their undoing when the first trials were carried out in the Dogger Bank area. In a modest sea the port paddle-wheel disintegrated.

With strengthened paddle-wheels fitted, the *Killingholme* set off for the appointed area with a full compliment of Schneiders. During the night two innocent looking fishing vessels approached and fired two torpedoes. One struck home, smashing a paddle-wheel, and causing *Killingholme* to limp back into harbour, never to be used in that role again.

The flying-boats used at *RNAS Killingholme* during the early part of the war had been the cumbersome White and Thompson 'Bognor Bloaters'. These were replaced by American designed Curtis flying-boats and their British derivatives, the Felixstowe F.2As. Two slipways were built to enable these aircraft to be launched and five 'aeroplane sheds' built to accommodate them when ashore (one of them later serving for many years as Grimsby bus station).

In July 1918 the air-station was handed over to the United States Navy by the newly-formed Royal Air Force. When the USN left, in January the following year, they presented the town of Immingham with the Stars and Stripes that had flown over the Killingholme air base. That flag now rests in Immingham museum with a section of the underside of a Curtis flying-boat. The original landing strip is now part of an industrial estate but one of the launching slipways remains, gently decaying by the water's edge.

24. Section of the hull of a Curtis flying boat from 1918 showing how, in those early days, they were indeed carvel built 'boats' with wings.

In addition to its major seaplane and flying boat base at Killingholme the RNAS also took over several areas designated as 'Emergency Landing Grounds'. In 1914 the Admiralty requisitioned land to the west of Cranwell village to be used as an airfield. Shortly after its acquisition it was decided that this base should be used to train pilots to fly aircraft, balloons, and airships; the training to be under the command of Commodore Godfrey Paine C.B., M.V.O. Clearly, such an important establishment had to have an appropriate name but the practise of naming shore bases in the manner of ships did not, at that time, exist. The answer was found in a floating pierhead at Chatham. Originally launched as an iron, steam-driven, floating battery in 1856 *HMS Thunderbolt* had been used in her ignominious pierhead position since 1873. In 1915 she was taken over as a depot ship for the RNAS and re-named *HMS Daedalus*. The Cranwell base, it was decided, would act as 'tender' to the Chatham hulk and no-one was going to object if, when the Commodore transferred his broad pennant to a Lincolnshire airstrip, he borrowed the title of the depot ship. Consequently, *HMS Daedalus* became among the first naval shore establishments to be given a ship's name.

HMS Daedalus was commissioned on 1 April 1916. Naval pilots, having completed their basic training at Crystal Palace, joined *Daedalus* after flying training at Eastchurch, Chingford, or Eastbourne; or, if they were to be balloon or airship pilots, at Roehampton or Wormwood Scrubs. *Daedalus* instructed them in advanced flying techniques including bombing and gunnery at nearby Freiston. In April 1918 the RAF took over, re-naming the base *RAF Cranwell*.

Today the RAF college at Cranwell has the mythological figure of *Daedalus* on its crest and roads named 'Airship' and 'Lighter than Air' serve as reminders of its early past. A minor revenge for the loss of *HMS Daedalus* to the Royal Air Force occurred many years later when, as the dawn broke on the day of their passing-out parade, the cadets woke to find that the aircraft on display had

25. *HMS Daedalus plaque: using both the naval crown and anchor and the eagle of the Royal Naval Air Service (later adopted by the RAF.*

'Fly Navy' painted along the side. The depot ship at Chatham served for many more years until rammed by a tug in 1948.

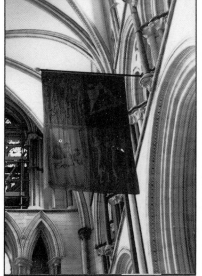

26. *The damaged Royal Standard in Lincoln Cathedral.*

When, in 1914, German cruisers bombarded Great Yarmouth and Lowestoft one of the items damaged was a Royal Standard. This had been flown only days before during a visit by King George V and had been awaiting collection in the office of Rear-Admiral Ellison at the local naval base. When he left the Navy to return to his Lincolnshire family home in 1930 Admiral Ellison presented the Standard to Lincoln Cathedral where it still hangs. The damage, however, is unlikely to have been caused through being holed by an 11' shell as is suggested by a nearby explanatory leaflet – it is much more likely to have been shrapnel damage. Nevertheless, the Standard remains possibly unique in being the only Royal Standard to be damaged in modern naval warfare.

27. *A Curtis flying boat similar to those flying from RNAS Killingholme.*

28. *An airship of the RNAS of the same type as those used at Cranwell (HMS Daedalus), here shown escorting a convoy.*

A Most Unfortunate Sailor

29. P. O. Harvey.

PETTY OFFICER A. E. HARVEY of Sutton Bridge was serving on board the elderly cruiser *HMS Hogue*. His ship, in company with the elderly cruisers *Aboukir* and *Cressy* patrolled the North Sea in an attempt to stop bombarding incidents such as had happened off Lowestoft. He had already seen action before the war in the Persian Gulf and off Somaliland and had narrowly escaped death ta the outbreak of war in August 1914 when the collapse of a wireless aerial threw him and another sailor into the sea. The Petty Officer was saved but the other man died.

At 6.30 am on the morning of 22 September 1914, a torpedo fired from the enemy submarine *U.9* struck the *Aboukir*. The ship heeled over immediately and, in less than half an hour, had sunk. Both the *Cressy* and the *Hogue* had moved close in to rescue the survivors when a torpedo exploded against the *Hogues* side. Harvey, blown clear of the ship by the blast, swam towards the *Cressy* as his old ship slipped beneath the waves.

Reaching the sole remaining cruiser left afloat, he was hauled aboard by willing hands only to feel for the second time that day the sickening lurch as yet another torpedo from *U.9* dealt the *Cressy* a mortal blow.

Once again the Petty Officer forund himself swimming for his life. This time he was rescued by a destroyer which brought him ashore and from where he was sent home to recover. He stayed for just one day before returning to the naval barracks eager to get back into the war.

It was not to be long before he was drafted to the *Clan McNaughton*, an armed merchant cruiser. In the following February the converted merchantman struck a mine and sank with the loss of all hands. The sea had at last claimed Petty Officer Harvey. The press report covering his death noted: A brave Lincolnshire sailor, he had more than his share of hardships.

COURAGE IN THE MARINES

30. Grantham's Lance-Corporal Walter Parker, V.C., R.M.,

O N 20 SEPTEMBER 1881 Mr and Mrs Parker of Agnes Street, Grantham, saw the birth of their son Walter. Thirty-three years later Walter Parker, by now a lance-corporal in the Royal Marines, had attracted the attention of his superiors by the manner in which he conducted himself under fire as a stretcher bearer in the Galipolli sector known as Anzac Cove. No-one was too surprised, therefore, when he was the first to respond to a call for volunteers to go and help the wounded in an isolated front-line trench. After organising his stretcher party he was making his way towards the 'jumping off' position when he was confronted by an Australian officer who demanded that Parker return to his own lines otherwise he would shoot him. Ignoring the drawn pistol in the officer's hand Parker pressed on until he could see the trench containing the wounded men. Between himself and the trench lay 400 yards of open ground constantly under the fire of the enemy. Gathering his small team together he gave the order to start running. They had not gone more than a few yards when a man was hit. Despite the incredible risks Parker stopped, turned, and arranged for the man to be stretchered back to safety. He then, to the cheers of the trenches behind him, began to race forward once more. Inevitably, a bullet found its mark and he crashed to the ground. Picking himself up, he ran on again only to have a second bullet smash through his body, but still he kept running. After what must have seemed like a lifetime Parker dropped into the forward trench – the only man still alive out of the party that had set off on their errand of mercy. Ignoring his own wounds, he began to treat the dreadful injuries of those in the trench, repeatedly having to stop in order to help fend off Turkish assaults. He was to be hit several more times before the order finally came to evacuate the trench – an operation in which he was seen to provide yet more leadership in such desperate circumstances. His wounds were so severe that he was never again able to serve in the war, but his bravery had earned him the Victoria Cross.

One weapon of war that might have saved Lance-Corporal Parker from having to pit himself against such fearsome odds began its life in an idea started by General Aston of the Royal Marine Brigade which had landed at Ostend in support of the Belgian Field Army in August 1914. A Royal Naval Air Service Squadron, temporarily short of aircraft for reconnaissance purposes, found itself unable to assist the Royal Marines as they withdrew towards Dunkirk. Aston, noting that the Squadron had a number of private cars at their base suggested to the Commanding Officer – Commander Samson – that these vehicles be used as reconnaissance units until more aircraft became available. Consequently, two of the cars were used for this purpose, one being fitted with a Maxim machine-gun. This instant mobility in the battle-zone (plus a brush with German cavalry which had the horsemen scattering in panic) led Samson to write a report to the First Lord of the Admiralty – Winston Churchill – recommending that vehicles be specially armoured and mounted with machine-guns. The idea struck home immediately with the First Lord and, in a very short time, eight squadrons of RNAS armoured cars had been raised and were soon serving in many theatres of the war as 'land torpedo-boats'.

31. The Hon. Francis McClaren, M.P.

One of the most eager to get involved in this new form of warfare was the Honorable Francis McLaren, M.P. the Member of Parliament for Spalding and – at twenty-nine – the youngest Liberal in the House. Through his Parliamentary connections he managed to secure for himself a commission as a Lieutenant in the Royal Naval Reserve and soon found

32. A British Royal Naval armoured-motorcar, September 1914.

33. A little later – but still Royal Navy.

34. Royal Navy officers driving a very early caterpillar-tracked vehicle. Hardly, as yet, a 'tank', but the elements of future developments can be seen.

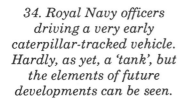

himself in command of a squadron of armoured cars at Gallipoli from where he telegraphed home that he was 'Well, Safe, Happy'.

The first ever combined air to ground operation took place during a probe against Lille when Flight Lieutenant Dalrymple-Clarke used flares to signal to the RNAS armoured cars beneath. Two years later Dalrymple-Clarke – as Squadron Commander – was killed during a training flight and was buried in Cranwell village churchyard. Despite several early successes, however, problems soon emerged.

It did not take long for the enemy to realise that such vehicles were, for the most part, confined to road and ready-made tracks. In an effort to beat this new menace the Germans began to dig trenches across roads thus barring the route to the cars. At this the First Lord demanded the development of special bridging materials to meet this challenge to the cars' mobility and – for a while – the carrying of stout wooden boards that could be removed and placed across the trenches, allowing the cars to be driven over, seemed to be the answer. As a further measure Admiral Sir Reginal Bacon suggested the development of an 'artillery tractor' with tracks capable of crossing trenches, whilst the Duke of Westminster (a Royal Naval Air Service officer who had turned his Rolls Royce into an armoured car) came up with the idea of a 1000 ton 'landship' that could cruise the battle-field impervious to the dreaded machine-gun fire that was causing such high casualties on all fronts. The First Lord responded to these ideas by ordering the Director of Naval Construction (Eustace Tennyson D'Eyncourt – born at Bayons Manor in the wolds village of Tealby) to found and chair a 'Landships Committee'. The Committee first met in February 1915 and it soon became clear that all the theories had to be put into practice and a manufacturer had to be found capable of handling heavy tracked machinery. Tennyson D'Eyncourt turned to his native county for the answer and chose Foster and Company, Engineers and Boilermakers at their Wellington Works, Lincoln (later work was to be extended to Marshalls of Gainsborough). Fosters, led by the innovative and energetic Willian Tritton and his team (William Rigby as chief draughtsman and Lieutenant Walter Wilson RN as the naval liaison officer) took to the idea and, within 37 days, had produced an armoured box on tracks weighing 15 tons and named 'Little Willie' (after the Kaiser's son). Whilst the principle remained good 'Little Willie' insisted on shedding its tracks whilst being put through its paces. As a result, a second design was rushed through, this time with the tracks encircling the entire armoured body. 'Big Willie' (as the new design had been named) was a great success with the Royal Navy supplying 6-pounder guns – complete with gun-crews – as the main offensive armament. However, despite being known as 'Land Cruisers', 'HM Caterpillar', or 'HM Landship Centipede' (or being nicknamed 'Tank' by Foster's workforce), the War Office began – in June 1915 – to take an interest in the new weapon. Eventually, the soldiers, backed by politicians senior to the First Lord and by Kitchener himself, took over the project – renaming 'Big Willie' as 'Mother' in the process. The Royal Navy responded by withdrawing the naval gun-crews and denying the army

6–pounder shells for the guns. Gradually, however, these problems were smoothed out and a Royal Navy sponsored and Lincolnshire built weapon went on to play a devastating role in future warfare. Today Tritton is remembered in Lincoln by having a road named after him, the White Hart Hotel (scene of the meetings between the Landships Committee and the Fosters' team) retains the Tank Room, and the Museum of Lincolnshire Life boasts one of the early tanks in its collection.

THE ANCASTERS AT SEA

The youngest son of the First Earl of Ancaster, Lieutenant-Commander the Honourable Peter Robert Heathcote Drummond Willoughby, had, like his illustrious ancester, the Earl of Lindsey, decided on a career at sea. In October 1914 he found himself on board *HMS Monmouth* sailing up the coast of Chile in search of the German Admiral Von Spee. The *Monmouth* was in company

35. HMS Monmouth

with *HMS Glasgow* and the Flagship of Admiral Sir Christopher Craddock, *HMS Good Hope*. The thoughts of all involved must have been somewhat mixed. Should they find the enemy it would be the first chance of the war for major warships to bring the enemy to action at sea. However, few could have failed to realise that compared to the ships under Von Spee's command they were woefully out-gunned and out-paced. Craddock had warned the Admiralty of the odds against his small squadron and a signal had been sent from London telling him that reinforcements were on the way but, before he had received that message, another one had come his way informing him that Von Spee was likely to be reinforced. Craddock immediately headed off towards the Chilean coast.

At twenty minutes past four in the afternoon of November 1st a lookout onboard *HMS Glasgow* spotted smoke on the horizon. The ship turned to investigate and soon the watchers on her decks could clearly make out the menacing shapes of two armoured cruisers followed by three light cruisers. The *Scharnhorst* led, followed by *Gneisenau, Leipzig, Dresden* and *Nurnberg*.

As the *Glasgow* turned with the German ships following in her wake she used her wireless to inform the Flagship of the presence of the enemy – the first time that the Royal Navy used wireless in a fleet action.

With the return of the *Glasgow* Craddock ordered his ships to form a 'line ahead' formation in parallel with the coast, their bows pointing southwards. Von Spee, with his much faster speed, also turned into the same formation and took his line so that it came between Craddock and the coast with the British ships about twelve miles on the starboard beam. At first this appeared to place the Germans at a disadvantage with their ships flooded by the light of the westerly sun but, as the sun began to set, darkess fell upon the Germans at the same time as the British ships were silhouetted against the sunset.

When he was satisfied that the lighting had clearly placed the British at a disadvantage Von Spee closed to within seven miles and opened fire with the sixteen 8.2 inch guns mounted by his largest ships. In reply the British could only use the two outdated 9.2 inch guns of *HMS Good Hope*. By the third German salvo both the *Monmouth* and the *Good Hope* were on fire and the forward gun of the *Good Hope* had been knocked out of action reducing the British response to a single gun.

The only answer was for the British to close with the enemy in order to bring into play their lighter guns but, with their extra turn of speed, the Germans continued to keep their distance. After ten minutes the damage to the *Monmouth* was such that she was forced to sheer out of the line, listing badly and with a fierce fire blazing around her fore-deck. Suddenly, as if in a rage to get at her tormentors, the *Monmouth* swung her bows towards the enemy and headed directly at their line, her small guns spitting impotently, their shells falling well short. This action was followed by the speedier flagship which also had flames flaring along the upper deck. Craddock may have decided to try and force the Germans onto the coast or may have been seeking an opportunity to launch torpedoes at the enemy – the answer will never be known. At ten minutes to eight a huge explosion ripped through the *Good Hope* sending her funnels circling into the air. Within seconds all trace of the ship and her ship's company had vanished. The Germans then turned their attention onto the *Monmouth* and, within minutes, the ship was down by the bows and staggering under the enemies' salvos. With darkness gathering around her the *Monmouth* tried to steam away from the Germans and moved slowly north-eastwards whilst signalling the *Glasgow* 'I want to get stern to sea as I am making water badly forward'. The *Glasgow* tried to close with the *Monmouth* to lend assistance but was driven off by the advancing Germans. Eventually it became clear that the only course of action open to the *Glasgow* was to escape into the darkness while she could and so, with heavy hearts, the ship left the scene with her lookouts watching as the night sky glowed with the glare of searchlights and the flash of guns as the *Nurnberg* came to within 6,000 yards of the *Monmouth* and sent 75 salvos into the reeling ship. With only a battered and blazing hulk in his searchlights the captain of the *Nurnberg* ordered his gunners to cease fire to allow the British ship to surrender. For three minutes an erie silence covered the scene with the only movement that the Germans could see being the fluttering of the *Monmouth's* battle ensigns. Then, with no sign of surrender forthcoming, a shattering salvo at point-blank range smashed into the British ship. She rolled over and disappeared beneath the waves. There were no survivors.

Von Spee sailed from the scene of the action intent on following the *Glasgow* and hunting down any other British ships in the region. He, and his ships, were to meet their own doom off the Falkland Islands five weeks later.

A memorial plaque to Lieutenant Commander Willoughby was placed in the family chapel at Grimsthorpe Castle – he had died within hours of his thirtieth birthday.

Lady Evelyn Willoughby, the sister of the First Earl of Ancaster, had married Major General Sir Henry Ewart and their only son, the 25 years old Lieutenant Victor Alexander Ewart, Royal Navy (Lieutenant-Commander Willoughby's cousin), had been appointed to *HMS Queen Mary* in time for the Grand Fleet's response to the German High Seas Fleet's venture into the North Sea.. Being one of the latest battle-cruisers, the *Queen Mary* had been placed under Vice-Admiral Sir David Beatty as part of his First Battle-Cruiser Squadron. Lieutenant Ewart was the turret officer of 'X' turret – the single turret on the quarterdeck – and was responsible for its twin 13.5 inch guns.

36. *Lieutenant V. A. Ewart, R.N.*

In the early afternoon of the 31 May 1916, having failed to find the enemy fleet, Beatty turned the First and Second Battle-Cruiser Squadrons and the Fifth Battle Squadron northwards to rejoin the main part of the Grand Fleet under Admiral Sir John Jellicoe. Just as the manouvre was completed Beatty was informed that one of his forward screen of cruisers had signalled 'enemy in sight'. He promptly ordered his ships to turn yet again and head towards the German ships. Unfortunately, due to smoke obscuring the signal flags, the Fifth Battle Squadron (four modern battleships) did not pick the signal up and continued northwards. Undeterred by the loss of the enormous fire-power disappearing northwards Beatty formed up 'line ahead' with his Flagship, *HMS Lion*, leading the *Princess Royal, Queen Mary, Tiger, New Zealand* and *Indefatigable*. Closing from the east was Vice-Admiral Hipper in his flagship *Lutzow* followed by the *Derfflinger, Seydlitz, Moltke,* and *Von der Tann*. At just past 3.45 p.m. the two sides opened fire almost simultaneously.

From the beginning the British ships found themselves with problems. Signal flags fluttering from the Flagship's halyards continued to be rendered unreadable by funnel smoke. Consequently instead of the British ships clearly understanding which of the enemy they were to engage, the second ship in the German line, the *Derfflinger*, found herself totally unmolested and able to pick her targets at leisure. The smoke that had caused confusion in signalling, in addition, thanks to a westerly breeze, obscured the view of their gun aimers – by four o'clock the Germans had scored fifteen hits compared to the British four. The *Lion* had had a lucky escape, thanks to the cold courage of a Royal Marine officer, who, after having his turret struck by a shell from the *Lutzow*, ordered the magazine doors closed and the magazine to be flooded, with himself inside. But the rear ship in the British line, *HMS Indefatigable*, was not so lucky. Hit by a salvo of shells, flames began to appear around her upper deck, then two more shells struck. For about thirty seconds nothing further happened until, with a huge flash, the ship exploded and disappeared, leaving only a vast cloud of black smoke to mark the spot.

Meanwhile, more hits had been scored on the *Lion* and so bad was the smoke pouring from the wounded ship that the gunnery officer of the *Derfflinger* could no longer make out his target. Accordingly, he transferred his attention to the third ship in the British line, *HMS Queen Mary* – already under fire from the *Seydlitz*. The *Queen Mary* had acquitted herself well during the battle. Her guns had been fired with great precision and, after turning her attention on to the *Derfflinger*, scored two hits which caused fires on her upper deck. Unfortunately, her next salvo produced a near miss creating huge columns of water which fell on her enemy and doused the fires. Then the *Derfflinger* found her range and went into rapid fire – a salvo of four eleven-inch shells leaving the ship every twenty seconds. At about five past four a *Derfflinger* salvo hit the *Queen Mary* with three shells. One of the projectiles smashed throught the roof of 'Q' turret (half-way along the ship's length). The flash from the explosion flared down to the magazine and a savage blast rocked throught the ship as cordite and shells exploded.

With the deck of 'X' turret badly warped from the explosion and the guns rendered useless the gunner's mate poked his head through a hole in the turret roof and saw that the upper deck was '. . . smashed out of all recognition and the ship had an awful list to port . . .'. Looking back into the turret he told Lieutenant Ewart about the situation. The turret officer had no choice but to shout the order: 'Clear the turret!'. The gunner's mate scrambled out through the turret roof followed by Lieutenant Ewart. They began to climb across the heavily sloping deck when '. . . suddenly he (Lieutenant Ewart) stopped and went back because he thought there was someone left inside . . .'. As Ewart disappeared once again into the turret an enormous explosion split the ship assunder sending a huge cloud of smoke into the air. On the flagship Beatty turned to his flag captain and remarked 'There seems to be something wrong with our bloody ships today'. Thirty seconds after the explosion *HMS Tiger* raced over to the spot where the *Queen Mary* had just been. There was no trace of the ship apart from wreckage still falling from the sky and, in the water, eighteen survivors out of the 1266 men of her ship's company. Among the survivors was the gunner's mate from 'X' turret, but no sign of Lieutenant

37. HMS Queen Mary explodes at Jutland

Ewart. The petty officer was later to write 'It makes me feel sore-hearted when I think of him and that fine crowd who were with me in the turret'. A memorial plaque to Lieutenant Ewart was placed in the chapel at Grimsthorpe castle alongside that of his cousin. The plaque records that: 'He surrendered his slender chance of life by returning into his turret to help his subordinate officers and men'.

Lieutenant Ewart's mother, after losing her husband, remarried into the Phipps family. Her son from this marriage – Simon – (Lieutenant Ewart's half-brother) later became the Bishop of Lincoln.

WAR IN THE ARCTIC

In the cold grey waters of the Norwegian sea on the morning of 17 October 1917, the destroyers *HMS Strongbow* and *HMS Mary Rose* kept a vigilant eye upon the merchant ships they were escorting. It was unexciting and unglamorous work but vital to the war effort. Little had been seen of the enemy's ships since the Battle of Jutland. Suddenly, the lookouts called out urgently to the bridge and all eyes peered out into the morning mist. Two heavily armed German cruisers loomed into view. The destroyers, with their much higher turn of speed, could have fled the scene and lived to fight another day. Instead, they pointed their bows at the enemy, hoisted battle-ensigns, and charged straight at the cruisers. There was just the chance that their light guns might get a lucky hit. If they could get close enough there were their torpedoes which, if one struck home, would prevent the enemy ship from closing with the convoy. But the Germans, irritated by this distraction, and keen to get to grips with the job of sinking the merchantmen, turned their heavy guns against the two small ships and opened fire. Within seconds the entire upper deck of *Strongbow* was a mass of twisted metal. A second salvo punched a hole in the destroyer's bows and she dived beneath the waters, her engines racing and tattered ensigns flying. *Mary Rose* had suffered the same fate. Sub-Lieutenant Arthur Pury-Cust of Belton House, near Grantham, was lost on board *HMS Strongbow*. A splendid bronze memorial, with a superb bas-relief of his ship, was placed in Belton Church to his memory.

Six months after the loss of the *Strongbow*, Lieutenant Charles Sinclair Wood RNR was killed at sea, aged 29 years. He is remembered with his brother, also lost in the Great War, by a plaque in St Botolph's church, Boston. The plaque bears at the top a copy of the Lincolnshire Regiment cap badge alongside a brass and enamel copy of a Royal Naval Reserve officer's cap badge.

38. Sub-Lieutenant Purey-Cust's memorial in Belton church

— AND THE WRENS ARRIVE —

During the war Lincolnshire had, almost by accident, found itself at the forefront of one of the greatest leaps forward in the history of the Royal Navy. With the establishment of the Navy's East Coast Command at Immingham it was discovered that there was a shortage of 'writers' (clerical and accounts ratings) – such men being required at sea. The Vice-Admiral in command con-sequently authorised the use of women clerks as early as November 1914. This novel, and successful, use of women in a naval environment encouraged the later formal creation of the Women's Royal Naval Service (WRNS or 'Wrens'). When this happened, one of the clerks – Miss M. Isemonger – was commissioned by the Admiral's Flag Captain as Divisional Director for the Humber Area.

Her first job was to organise a telephone watch-keeping system for the Signal Station at Immingham Dock. This was followed by the replacement of naval officers by Wrens in the nearby Coding Office. Soon Wrens were oiling and cleaning torpedoes, adjusting gyroscopes, and maintaining searchlights and hydrophones. Other, local, women 'of the rougher type' were considered by Miss Isemonger to be 'unfitted' for entry into the fledgling Service thanks to their fish docks 'customs and mode of life'. However, they did splendid work in cleaning mines, priming depth charges, and the repair of wire anti-submarine nets having 'learnt to splice as neatly as any sailor.'

39. A 'Wren' at work in the torpedo sheds at Immingham.

MANY DID NOT RETURN

40a. Immingham church wall plaque.

THROUGHOUT THE WAR many naval memorials and graves made final homes in Lincolnshire. The church at Immingham had formed a particular link with the Royal Navy through the nearby Naval Base. Many men and ships are remembered on the marble plaques on its walls. The Naval Base church gave it their lectern, pulpit, and other church furniture. The Naval Base also presented the church with a large white ensign – now in Immingham museum. In the churchyard many graves bear witness to the local naval involvement. Here can be found a stoker who died on board *HMS Chester* at Jutland – the ship in which Boy First Class John ('Jack') Cornwell won the Victoria Cross in the same action and who was buried at

40b. A group of wall plaques in Immingham church.

41. Private T. H. Jackson

nearby Grimsby prior to being moved to his home town – East Ham, London. Private Jackson of the Royal Marines also lies here after his death on the Zeebruge Mole on St George's Day 1918 as does Lieutenant Arthur Dickinson who had been created a Chevalier de la Legion D'Honneur by the French 'for distinguished services rendered during the war'.

The War Memorial at Boston carries, among the names carved into its sides, a sad reminder that warfare had become no longer a normally male only affair. The Women's Royal Naval Service did not have many casualties prior to their de-commissioning in 1919 but one of their number, Elizabeth Beardshall, is listed amongst Boston's war dead.

At the end of the war Blyton church gathered to itself a collection of flags from all the Allies as a memorial to the village dead. Among the flags still decorating the church is a White Ensign presented by Admiral Lord Beatty – it had seen action at Jutland.

Due to the Royal Naval Air Service being absorbed into the Royal Air Force, naval activity in the county during the inter-war years was limited mainly to ship visits to Grimsby. The battleship *HMS Resolution* spent three days at the port in January 1924. Sadly the occasion was not a happy one as the day before her arrival the huge ship had rammed and sunk Submarine *H.42* with the loss of all hands.

42. Lieut. Arthur Dickinson

HMS GRIMSBY

Nine years later the people of Grimsby were delighted to have a ship of their own. There had been a requisitioned trawler named *HMT Grimsby* in the Great War (First World war 1914 – 1918) but the new *Grimsby* was to be a smart 990 ton sloop. So proud of her was the Town that on her first visit,

43. HMS Grimsby

in June 1934, the Council voted an increase in the allowances for the Mayor of £100 in order to cover the extra expenses they were determined to incur during her stay. To mark the visit even further the Town presented their ship with three silver trays. The ship's part in the coming war was to be small but distinguished. Having already earned the battle honours 'Greece 1941', 'Crete 1941', and 'Libya 1941' she was sunk by enemy aircraft off Tobruk whilst defending a convoy. The silver trays, however, survived and are now on permanent loan to the Borough Council.

THE SECOND WORLD WAR

O N SUNDAY 3 SEPTEMBER 1939 visitors to Butlin's holiday camp at Skegness saw a comedian – Izy Bon – top the bill at the camp concert. The following day the Royal Navy requisitioned the camp and re-named it *HMS Royal Arthur*. For the next five years it was to be the Royal Navy's Initial Training Base with over 4,500 men under training at any one time. Run on the same principles as a sea-going warship *HMS Royal Arthur* had 'duty watches', a quarterdeck (ex sandpits) and a sick-bay (ex Tyrolean beer garden). The York, Gloucester, and Kent dining rooms became respectively the Forecastle, Top, and Quarterdeck Divisions. The Viennese dance hall, which had once swayed to the music of Victor Sylvester, now became the armoury, and morse code was taught in the Palm Lounge. Hammocks were slung in the chalets whilst petty officers rode around on yellow bicycles originally intended for hire to holidaymakers. New Entries were warned in a welcoming handbook that orders were to be received with 'Aye aye, Sir' and not with 'Righto!' Lord Haw Haw declared *HMS Royal Arthur* sunk with all hands and the Luftwaffe tried to substantiate his claim by dropping a total of 52 bombs on the camp.

This *HMS Royal Arthur* was in fact the second of that name the first having been a 'protected cruiser' laid down in Portsmouth in 1890, launched on 28th February the following year, and commissioned

44. *The Theatre of Butlin's Holiday Camp now known as the Gaiety Theatre of Funcoast World.*

on 2nd March 1893. Although a 7,700 ton vessel of 369 feet in length and with a complement of 544 men (and armed with one 9.2", twelve six-pounders, and two 18" torpedo tubes) she was somewhat smaller (and, with a top speed of 19.5 knots more nimble) than the Skegness *HMS Royal Arthur!* She was sold after the First World War in 1921 and finally broken up in Germany. Some time after the camp was handed back to Billy Butlin in 1946 a further *HMS Royal Arthur* was commissioned at Corsham in Wiltshire as a leadership training school.

45. Junior Probationary Electrical Mechanic Hillebrandt, M.A., D/MX105551 at H.M.S. Royal Arthur September 1942. The rows of identical chalets from the pre-war holiday camp days, in which the new entrants lived, can be seen stretching away behind him.

46. A chalet from the H.M.S. Royal Arthur days preserved as 'a building of historical interest' in the present Fun Coast World.
(Photograph taken by M.A.Hillebrandt in May 1988 at the first Royal Arthur reunion.)

As, during the wartime years, something like a quarter of a million men passed through the Skegness *HMS Royal Arthur* there are still many men (and a few women who were on the staff of the camp as 'Wrens') who remember the greeting which met them as a reminder of – and much more applicable to – the holiday camp days:

'OUR TRUE INTENT IS ALL FOR YOUR DELIGHT'

Despite the 'less than holiday-like' sojourn experienced by those who did pass through the training establishment, the comradeship and nostalgic memories were renewed for about 150 men and women (some being spouses) who reassembled there in 1988 at what is again a holiday complex but now known as 'Funcoast World'. As a result of that first reunion (*Fig. 47.* see below) *The HMS Royal Arthur Association* was founded and there are presently some 600 members who meet at Skegness annually. They have been accorded a civic welcome and are likely to continue to meet there annually for

47. Photograph taken by M.A. Hillebrandt at the first reunion of the former H.M.S. Royal Arthur 'crew' and trainees, including some Wrens who were on the strength of the base, and also some spouses. It was from this reunion that the H.M.S. Royal Arthur Association was formed.

(The Embassy Centre is in the centre of Skegness – about two miles from the camp – and not part of the former Butlin's Holiday Camp, now Funcoast World.)

many years to come. In the present 'Funcoast World' there is one of the wartime chalets still preserved as 'A Building of Historic Interest' *(Fig. 46).*

Two other temporary naval bases were set up in Lincolnshire during the Second World War. Immingham was chosen as the base of the admiral commanding the Humber defences. The local dry dock did sterling services in repairing battle-damaged naval ships, one of which was *HMS Kelly*, her commanding officer – Captain the Lord Louis Mountbatten – staying at the town's County Hotel.

In September 1942 Boston saw the establishment of *HMS Arbella* (named after the lady who had sailed with early settlers to America – see page 14) in part of what had once been the workhouse. Little of this building now remains although a small part of the entrance block and facade is presently preserved — see *Fig. 48.* The Ensign flown by *Arbella* during the war can be seen in Boston's St. Botolph's church (the 272 feet high 'Boston Stump' – a landmark to seafarers in The Wash for more than 500 years), preserved 'in glad

48. *All that now [1991] remains of HMS Arbella. Originally built as a Poor Law Institution (workhouse) in the middle of the nineteenth century it has, since being de-requisitioned by the Royal Navy, served as a school, a home for the elderly, a temporary home for a number of Asian families expelled from Uganda by Idi Amin in the early 1970s, and various temporary local authority purposes. The main buildings were demolished about the end of the 1970s and replaced by the large circular grain silos visible in the picture for the immediately adjacent dock. The buildings still standing have a preservation order on them as buildings of historic interest (because of their 19th century origins — not because of their Royal Naval associations).*

rememberance'.

The minesweeper, *HMS Boston*, the seventh Royal Navy ship to bear that name, was launched in 1940 (see *Fig. 49*). In the following year, the Town and Corporation presented their ship with its bell. The *Boston* had a busy war, taking part in operations in the Atlantic, in Malta convoys, and the invasions

49. HMS Boston (the seventh Royal Navy ship to bear the name).

50. One of the Gainsborough built midget submarines. The two men on
the deck of the submarine give an idea of the size of the craft.

51. The only remaining midget submarine now in the Submarine Museum at HMS Dolphin, Gosport, Hants.

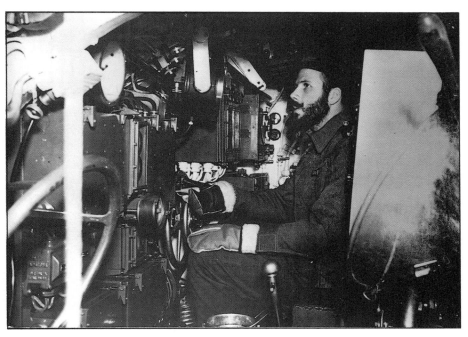

52. This photograph helps to give some idea of the tiny size and consequent cramped conditions inside a midget submarine.

of Sicily and Normandy. She was sold and broken up in 1948.

The engineering firm Marshalls of Gainsborough were already producing guns for the Royal Navy when, early in 1943, they were approached by the Admiralty and asked if they could manufacture midget submarines ('X' craft). With Marshalls showing they had the skill and capacity for such a task the job got under way and soon the 'X' craft produced at Gainsborough were closing with the enemy. *X.24* attacked enemy shipping in the Norwegian port of Bergen blowing up the 780 ton freighter *Barenfels* and putting the important coaling wharf out of action for the remainder of the war. Bergen was revisted by *X.24* in September 1944. Using the mast of the sunken *Barenfels* as a marker the tiny craft dropped her explosive side-charges under the harbour's floating dock. As the submarine escaped to the sea down the connecting fjord the charges exploded, wrecking the dock and badly damaging two ships secured alongside. The sole survivor of Gainsborough's 'X' craft, *X.24,* is now on exhibition at the Royal Navy's Submarine Museum at Gosport.

George Wilfred Holt was born at Sturton by Scawby on 25 July 1912. A fortnight before his thirty-first birthday he found himself sweeping towards the south-east coast of Sicily in command of the 503rd Landing Craft Flotilla. He had already seen much action including the landings at Dieppe a year earlier but his actions in the Sicily landing earned him the Distinguished Service Cross: 'For gallant and distinguished services and untiring devotion to duty in operations which led to the capture of Sicily by Allied Forces'. Sadly, the wounds he received on that occasion led to his death two months later. His memorial can be seen in Broughton Church. Beneath the carving of a naval officer's cap badge are the words 'He wears immortal honours and is proud, with those who fought for England, and passed content'.

Yet again, with the ending of the war, as after the First World War, the names of the county's naval dead shared space with their soldier and airmen comrades on the war memorials in the county's towns and villages. All marked a personal tragedy for families and friends so, perhaps, one can speak for all. On 25 November 1941, *HMS Barham*, greviously wounded by a torpedo off the coast of Egypt, rolled slowly onto her side. Suddenly, to the horror of helpless onlookers, she was ripped apart in a savage explosion. Among the 862 men who died at that moment was 25 years old Bill Fowler of Lincoln. His death is recorded by his mother on a block at the base of Lincoln's War Memorial – the wording continues on to read '. . . Also his Dad, killed in 1918, aged 25'.

AFTER THE SECOND WORLD WAR

THE ARMAMENTS FIRM BMARC on Springfield Road, Grantham had, during the Second World War, produced 20 mm. cannon for Spitfires and their sea-going equivalents, the Seafires. With the introduction of the Seafury after the war, the successful weapon was transferred to the new aircraft. During the summer of 1952, at the height of the Korean war, Lieutenant P 'Hoagy' Carmichael, flying a Seafury, shot down a MiG-15. It was the first time that a piston engined aircraft had emerged victorious in a fight with a jet engined aircraft – and it was a gun from Grantham that helped to make history.

The Admiralty, in the 1950s, decided to honour the county by naming several new ships after its villages. Bassingham gave its name to an inshore minesweeper, whilst Leverton, Santon, Fiskerton, and Belton gave their names to coastal minesweepers (the latter two being built by Doig's of Grimsby). Santon was sold, in 1967, to the Argentinian navy as the *Chubit*. There is no evidence that she took any part in any subsequent conflict concerning the Falkland Islands.

On 23 June 1956 the stained glass windows in the Seaman's chapel of Lincoln Cathedral were unveiled by Admiral of the Fleet Viscount Cunningham of Hyndhope. The windows depict Smith, Lady Arbella, Banks, Bass, Flinders and Franklin. Viscount Cunningham also presented the Chapel with a pair of brass dolphins from his wartime flagship *HMS Queen Elizabeth*. Other Royal Naval mementos include the bell of *HMS Tasman* (never actually used by a ship of that name as the vessel it was intended for changed its name to *HMS Talent* prior to launch); the White Ensign of *HMS Lapwing*, a destroyer that had taken part in the Battle of Jutland in 1916; and the White Ensign of *HMS Lance*, a ship which created havoc in the Mediterranean under Viscount Cunningham. Among the *Lances's* officers had been Lieutenant Charles Jenny, RNVR. When the ship had been hit by enemy bombs at Malta he grabbed the White Ensigns that flew at the masthead and stern as the ship sank beneath him. At the end of the war he presented one Ensign to the Cathedral, the second eventually accompanied his cap, sword and medals on his coffin at his funeral service at Scampton church in January 1992. The First Lieutenant of the *Lance* – Lieutenant-Commander (later Admiral Sir) Godfrey Styles – wrote of him that '. . . he was of English Oak, even of Lincolnshire Oak, and with the courage.' During his final years Lieutenant-Commander Jenny was the President of the Lincoln Sea Cadets and never missed an opportunity to inform any young person considering a career in the Royal Air Force that it meant 'a step down on the social ladder.'

The Cathedral's Seaman's chapel was not the first reminder of the county's sea-going heritage in that great building. In 1732, one 'R Reading' scratched a splended graffito of a fully rigged sailing man-of-war into the stonework.

THE THIRD *HMS LINCOLN*

When the first three Type 61 frigates had been built they had been given the names *Salisbury*, *Chichester*, and *Llandaff*. The fourth, much to the pleasure of the city, was to be called *Lincoln*. Laid down in 1955 and launched in 1959, *HMS Lincoln* was completed the following year. She was armed with a twin 4.5 inch mounting forward, a twin 40 m.m. mounting aft, and a 'Squid' anti-submarine mortar. Eventually, Seacat missiles were to be fitted. She had twin screws powered by eight diesel engines giving her a speed of 24 knots — sufficient speed for her intended role as a convoy escort. *Lincoln* did sterling

53. The third HMS Lincoln turning to starboard at speed.

work, mainly in 'showing the flag' roles until the early 1970s when she was placed in reserve. She was called out in 1976 to take part in the 'Cod War' before returning, once again, to the Reserve. *Lincoln*, by now hopelessly outdated, was sold and broken up in 1983. Her bell now rests in Lincoln Guildhall as does a splendid silver model of her made in honour of her launch. She had been the third to bear the name. The first had been a 48 gun 'fourth rate' launched in 1695 which had foundered in 1703. The second had been a 'Lend-Lease' destroyer — *USS Yarnall* — on loan from the US Navy. After a

54. *The second HMS Lincoln, one of the 50 old, but invaluable, destroyers lent to Britain by The USA in November 1940 in exchange for bases in the West Indies. The ship is 'dazzle painted' (camouflaged) to confuse enemy gunners.*

year she was loaned to the Norwegians and then to the Russians who re-named her *Drozni*. After the war she returned to the US Navy and was broken up in 1952.

Despite the loss of the *Lincoln* (and of the minesweepers, the last of which had gone by the end of the 1970s), the county was not to be left without a ship of its own. *HMS Brocklesby* was launched in 1982 as one of the most modern minehunters anywhere in the world and is currently serving with the Fleet. A previous *Brocklesby* – a 'Hunt' class destroyer launched in 1940 – gave distinguished service before being broken up in 1968. Her battle honours included; English Channel 1942-43, Dieppe 1942, Sicily 1943, Salerno 1943, Atlantic 1943, and Adriatic 1944.

Sadly, the need for a strong Royal Navy was emphasised by the Argentinian invasion of the Falkland Islands in 1982. Lincoln-born helicopter pilot, Lieutenant-Commander R. E. Wilkinson, having decided to move back to his home town, was less than pleased after a hard day moving in to hear a knock on his new front door. The knock had come from a policeman who told him (the telephone

55. *Lieut.-Cdr. R. E. Wilkinson, RN, wearing the oak leaf clasp for 'mentioned in des-patches' on the South Atlantic medal ribbon.*

56. Atlantic Conveyor — on fire off the Falklands, 25th May 1982. The order to abandon ship was given ninety minutes after the Exocet attack. The ship sank three days later when under tow by a tug. The loss of twelve men killed and many invaluable stores including all but one of the Chinook heavy carrying helicopters, six Wessex and one Lynx helicopters together with many thousands of tons of stores was one of the most significant losses of the campaign. From a painting by Robert Taylor on loan to The Fleet Air Arm Museum at Yeovil by The Military Gallery, Bath.

having yet to be connected) that he had to report to a new ship at Devonport in two days time. Five weeks later Lieutenant-Commander Wilkinson found himself swimming for his life in the icy waters of the South Atlantic. His ship – the *Atlantic Conveyor* – had been bit by an Exocet missile probably aimed originally at the nearby aircraft carrier, *HMS Hermes*. As the ship begain to sink he established communication with helicopters from the *Hermes*, directing them to people in the water with only the weak light from a setting sun to assist him. Despite the risk of the ship sinking beneath him he remained at his post until, after 90 minutes, the order was given to abandon ship. He jumped clear and spent the next hour in the water before being picked up in the dark by *HMS Brilliant*. When Lieutenant-Commander Wilkinson collected his Falkland Islands medal it came with the ribbon emblazoned with the bronze oak-leaf awarded as a result of his being 'Mentioned in Despatches' during the loss of the *Atlantic Conveyor*.

A further narrow escape came his way in September 1990 when, as the Deputy Director of Recruiting for the East Region, he was forced to delay his arrival at his office as he checked on a car being repaired at a nearby garage. As he arrived at the garage he heard a loud explosion followed by the sound of shattering glass – the IRA had placed a bomb on the roof of his office.

Since the Falklands conflict the armament of ships has been looked at closely with, among other results, BMARC of Grantham (now part of Astra Holdings) currently supplying the Royal Navy with 20 mm. and 30 mm. guns.

Of the Royal Navy itself, little remains in the county. Lincoln has a

Recruiting Office, naval officers are trained at the Central Flying School (now back in the county, at RAF Scampton), and, when operational programmes permit, ships still call at Grimsby, Boston, and Immingham.

But, while the lure of the sea still exerts a hold on men — and nowadays, women — the county of Lincolnshire will, as it always has done, contribute its part in the seaward defence of the country.

As a memorial in Gunby church has, etched in marble:

"PRAY NOT FOR YOUR CHILDREN AN EASY VOYAGE,
BUT A GALLANT FARING IN THE HIGH SEAS"

In August 1992, after this book had been prepared for press, the author returned from a further exploration of King William Island and provided the following preliminary note as a result of that journey. Any further information will depend on properly supported excavation of the site found. This in turn will depend on official support and will, in any case, be restricted to the Arctic 'summer'.

In 1992 a further expedition by the author, this time solo, reached the barren north-west coast of King William Island. In addition to casting doubt on the official location of Victory Point (Commander James Rose's furthest point reached in 1830) and identifying Franklin's 'Drift Calculator' on the northern tip of the island, a possible major discovery was made on 14 July.

Two large mounds, similar in every way to British burial mounds or 'barrows', were found to the south of Cape Felix. When examined by experts these mounds could prove to be the final resting place of Franklin and those men of his expedition who had died prior to Captain Crozier's attempt to reach safety by heading south.

INDEX

Page numbers in **bold thus** and underscored indicate an illustration

82.